A Journey Into the Self

A Journey Into The Self

THE MULTI-DIMENSIONAL NATURE OF BEING HUMAN

George E. Lockett

Cover photo by Mark Land—Artist

2006

A Journey Into the Self

CONTENTS

EDITOR'S PREFACE

What is this book going to do for YOU?

For those who are seeking a complete energetic makeover, as you read it you will feel a stirring and awakening in the depths of your heart.

For those who have questions about Shifts in Consciousness, Energy Balancing and Healing within the body, you will find clear answers.

It begins as an autobiography, describing vividly the emotions and experiences that HealerGeorge encountered on his spiritual journey.

It goes on to describe the many benefits received from sixth sense experiences of contact with Angels, Guides and Spirit Helpers, out-of-body experiences, connection to the Universal Life Force and how we can use this in our daily life.

I experienced major changes in my own perception of my life simply through contact with the book. I also clearly felt the presence of a group of many lighted humans and angels who have contributed to the information in the book.

May this book bring dazzling light and showers of grace to your own life's journey.

GLOSSARY

Below is an alphabetical list of the key words used, and their meaning in the context of the book.

Abundance—*The experience of having enough of the different aspects of life, which includes money, love, etc.*

Angel—*An unseen impulse of energy that is intelligent and can travel, taking messages and requesting actions to take place.*

Aura—*The multi-layered electromagnetic field of awareness which surrounds and permeates the body, creating an energy structure of consciousness on which the physical body is built and co-ordinated. This is also sometimes referred to as an Energy Field.*

Broadband—*Multidimensional connection to different aspects of the universe, which flows without resistance and connects planets and stars across the full electromagnetic spectrum.*

Central Sun (see also Sun)—*The core of our universe, which has physical form but mainly co-ordinates through its unseen energy presence of consciousness and intelligence that unites all aspects into the oneness of life.*

Chakra—*One of a number of energy vortices (i.e. energy moving with a spiralling motion) within the body which receive and radiate different frequencies of the electromagnetic spectrum. These vortices criss-cross and interact with each other, producing a multi-layered matrix, like radio tuners, receiving and giving out the different frequencies of energy impulse between people and the universe around us.*

Consciousness (see also Group Consciousness)—*The field of self-aware impulses of intelligence that form the aura of the body. Note that this is multi-layered and multi-dimensional in nature. The subconscious mind is formed of the layers of intelligence which the awareness still needs to realize and make conscious.*

Digestive Fire—*In Ayurveda, a science of conscious living from India that goes back 3 millennia, the Sanskrit word for fire—Agni—denotes the digestive and metabolic "fire" produced by the doshas (the archetypical forces of creation) that grabs the essence of nourishment from food, feelings, and thoughts and transforms it into a form your body can use.*

Energy (see also New Energy)—*That which the universe is made of in its many forms, both manifest (physical) and unmanifest (subtle), which displays both consciousness and awareness and is constantly evolving.*

Group Consciousness (see also Consciousness)—*The level of awareness between people. It can be defined at the level of the Family, Housing Estate or Town, Country, World: it sets the mindset, i.e. belief systems, of the people within that Group Consciousness.*

Guide—*Spirit entity that may be seen with clairvoyance, or may be felt—or you may just know it is there—and whose purpose is to help you on your path of life, without interfering with any of your choices.*

Higher Self (see also Self)—*The unmanifest, unchanging, eternal aspect of your Self that is sometimes referred to as Spirit, or Universal Energy, or God.*

Inner Self (see also Self)—*The unmanifest nature of the Space or Vacuum referred to in Quantum Physics. The Inner Self is reached by transcending your physical body through dropping down the layers of energy to finer and finer levels: i.e. through the organs of the body into the cells, down into the molecules and atoms, and transcending physical matter altogether into the realms of Spirit or Space.*

Karma—*Just means action. We can build good karma by performing life-supporting action or bad karma by destroying life. We transcend the influence of past karma by connecting with our Higher Self and aligning our energy with that of the universe.*

Kundalini—*A warm, liquid, magnetic energy which rises up the spinal cord.*

Light Body—*An energy body that you have at a higher level, closer to your soul. It underlies all your chakras and connects their sources to the Silence or Space.*

Mantra—*A sound that is charming to the mind and which, when repeated over and over with the body sitting comfortably, leads the mind naturally to quieter fields of awareness and slows the brainwaves. Affirmations can be used in a similar way to create a certain influence in your life.*

Moment (see also Now Moment)—*The only time that is real in our life is the Moment of Now. Things in the future have not been created yet, and things in the past are just a memory. You can also say that everything is happening Now, and future and past do not exist except in our concept of time; though the Now can evolve over time by becoming more conscious of its Self.*

Nature—*That which flows from the Universal Life Force and has evolved over time. Nature is the display of intelligence which flows from the unmanifest level of creation into the plant and animal kingdoms and which we see as the natural world around us.*

New Energy (see also Energy)—*A shifting of human consciousness from the level of the individual, to the individual being aware of the whole of life as an aspect of their Self: this wholeness of life forms the basis of their consciousness and they make decisions on the basis of the whole.*

New Spirituality (see also Spirituality)—*A move towards expressing the* oneness of life, and tracing all religions to a common source of inspiration; it is bringing forth the understanding of the wholeness of life and its interconnectedness.

Now Moment (see also Moment)—*Being present, i.e. fully aware of all your senses and their connectedness to the environment around you, in a state of restful alertness: the mind fully connected and focussed on what is happening Now.*

Omniverse—*The multidimensional nature of this universe—connected to all the other universes, in a web of energy folding back on itself from the field of unmanifest Space, flowing outwards in the ever-expanding diversity with which life expresses itself.*

Oversoul (see also Soul)—*The collective souls of the universe, as a subtle mani-festation of group consciousness or interconnectedness of life, which can be consulted deep in your heart for advice or guidance.*

Self (see also Higher Self, Inner Self)—*The soul of the individual, which is a part of the whole Universal Life Force.*

Soul (see also Oversoul and Soul Purpose)—*A unique individual vibration that creates the first sprouting of consciousness out of the unmanifest field of neutral energy which gives rise to physical creation of the human body.*

Soul Purpose (see also Soul)—*Is like the swell on the ocean. Your life is the individual wave, but the swell also carries you along and has a deeper effect on your life.*

Source / Source Energy—*The unmanifest level of potential energy which un-derlies physical creation and that is the source of its being. A sorcerer, wizard or shaman is someone who can create out of this unmanifest source energy at will.*

Spirit—*Is the unseen aspect of conscious awareness, which exists as electromagnetic plasma of the soul of a person whose body has been dropped, and continues to flow their ener-gies in the Spirit world. This term can also refer to the collective soul or oversoul.*

Spirituality (see also New Spirituality)—*The waking up of human aware-ness to its spiritual nature and unmanifest being. It is the growth in conscious awareness of the wholeness of life and its collective intelligence and being.*

Sun (see also Central Sun)—*Sun is the Life Force and the Source of Fire in the five elements which are needed to create life on Earth. Its feminine counterparts are the Moon and Venus, which reflect the light of the Sun.*

Yogi (man) or Yogini (woman)—*An enlightened person: a person who has realized their inner connectedness to the whole universe.*

I dedicate this book to all humans and angels—both incarnate and discarnate—who are helping the evolution of Planet Earth and all her life forms.

I thank all of you who have worked with me through telepathy, on the level of consciousness, to co-create this book.

Those of you of whom I am not yet aware, please bring yourselves to my conscious awareness, so I can thank you individually. Namasté.

FOREWORD

Journey into the Self by George E Lockett

This book is about a personal journey. This journey took place on Planet Earth, the expression of just another blip of consciousness which makes up our planet.

The place is not important, as this is the description of a journey into your Self; in reality an awakening of the consciousness of the whole universe, by a journey into the conscious mind of the individual.

This awakening is a process of self-knowledge—a turning back of consciousness on its Self. The process takes place on the level of the individual but in reality each individual is part of a much larger system—a universe awakening.

I hope you enjoy this journey as much as I have enjoyed living and writing about it.

We are all blessed with love. Go out and shine your light to the world.

George E Lockett

INTRODUCTION

Welcome to a new world, a world of make-believe that may just change the universe around you. Lots of people ask themselves, what is the purpose of life? What is my destiny? Do I have a predetermined purpose, which reflects my previous karma from past lives? How will I know what is right and wrong?

- What does depth mean when looking at the human physiology?
- What are the layers of consciousness?
- How do the two interact?
- What is the interaction between the aura and consciousness?
- How do the chakras help in the raising of personal frequency?

The answers to these and many more questions I hope to make clear in this book.

This book is not something to follow or to practise: it is just an understanding, one of many which create the great diversity of the planet Earth and our universe in which we live.

I feel very privileged to have been given the vision of life itself, reflecting on itself, in so many different ways. I am sure that each one of you that reads this knowledge can add your own experience to it and see the world in your own unique way.

There are many synchronies in life. I feel that you have been drawn to read this book: it is not a coincidence, but one of those synchronies that may just change your life forever.

It is better to know and understand and live in awareness. I bring this knowledge to you with love and great compassion.

You are all blessed.

PART I

My Spiritual Journey

A look at events in HealerGeorge's life which led up to his current life journey

My spiritual journey began in 1977, when I was 22, taking a Business Studies course. Exam time was upon me quite suddenly and I was finding it difficult to sleep. Instead of tossing and turning I decided to make use of my restlessness and began looking through the local paper.

An advert jumped out of the page at me. There, staring back at me, was an introductory lecture on Transcendental Meditation as taught by Maharishi Mahesh Yogi.

I attended the introductory talk in Ormskirk, Lancashire and later learned the technique of meditation in Southport. Little did I know at that time what this advertisement was going to bring to my path: the changes—let alone the lessons—which I was to attain from this wonderful lecture! My story continues. . .

The following summer I attended a weekend course at a spiritual retreat. The course leader suggested that I consider going to Switzerland on "work-study". This involved working in return for food, accommodation and credit towards courses, with the opportunity to see and hear the Maharishi giving lectures in the evening.

How could I pass up such an opportunity? Turned out, I stayed in Switzerland for the next three years. This was a very enjoyable time of my life with people of my own age, all with a common interest.

The most noticeable thing I remember was the power of the atmosphere. By that I mean the spiritual energy that was created by 3,000 people all practising meditation in close proximity to each other.

I started to notice the advantages of this energy in terms of attracting to oneself what the environment around one needed.

At the time, I was in charge of maintenance for all the accommodation of the residential courses and I wanted to design a form for people to report maintenance problems. I decided that this would be very useful and started to go about my day's work.

As I was walking down the corridor, I was asked to have a look at one of the printing presses. I managed to fix it and the person in charge of printing said, is there anything I can do for you in exchange?

So I explained about the forms I wanted printed and showed him a sample. He said, come back later in the afternoon and I should have them ready.

I walked a little further down the corridor and, just as I was passing the Communications Office, the door opened and a bag of rubbish was just being put outside. On top of the rubbish was a clear plastic display case with two compartments, which was ideal for displaying the forms.

I set up the display case next to the mailboxes, for the whole site, later labelling them and displaying the forms. I watched this idea materialize effortlessly and naturally as though it were all co-ordinated by a greater mind than, at the time, I thought my mind was.

That is really why I thought this a special time. Life was magical! Problems just did not seem to exist; life flowed effortlessly from one achievement to the next. I did not need to worry about money as all my needs were taken care of by the organization.

After I had lived in Switzerland for about two and a half years I became friendly with one of the cooks named Dorothea. During our free days we would go off walking in the mountains and we had a lovely time together.

Relationships within the organization were frowned upon and very soon we were found out. Dorothea was sent to Arosa, a ski resort up in the mountains, to work in one of the course hotels.

Though, as it happened, I was still getting the "support from nature" and, two weeks later, I too was sent to Arosa, to repair the damages in the hotels as each course finished.

I did not realize at the time, but this relationship was to play a big part in my evolution. As I got to Arosa I went to see Dorothea. This was not very straightforward as the Movement had its own police force, called the "wims", who guarded the entrances to the hotels.

The hotels were either male only or female only and it was the wims' job to keep the two apart. Well, being a young male myself, I used my creativity and, as Dorothea's room was on the first floor, I took advantage of a drainpipe that descended alongside the balcony and we spent the night together.

The next morning I left her room at 6 a.m., before everyone was awake, and returned to my own room. As I was entering my hotel I met a man on the entrance steps and one look said a thousand words, as I was probably looking quite rough with bags under my eyes.

It was not until three months later that I realized the significance of that chance meeting on the steps of the hotel. I had finished my three years' work-study and now could go on the course I had been working for.

You have probably already guessed: the man on the steps was my course leader.

By this time Dorothea had returned to Germany, where she lived with her parents. As you can imagine, during my course I was lovesick nearly all the time. My weight almost halved and I found the routine of the course very tiring.

Though on the spiritual side I think this was meant to be, as I found my intuition and powers of telepathy became very acute.

I found I could feel the meaning in the words as Dorothea wrote to me. It was as though I were in the room looking at her as she wrote her letters to me. I always knew word for word what she had written, and reading the letters just confirmed what I already knew was there.

During this time my consciousness became very clear and, with Dorothea's help, my sixth sense was developed, as we would go off astral travelling together at night in our dreams. We would dream about the future after the course was finished.

I also noticed my sixth sense developing in other ways. I noticed that if I shook hands with someone, I was able to read their thoughts and know what their intentions were. This seemed to explain the tradition of clinching business deals with a handshake.

Dorothea came to see me in England when my course was over. We both found that I had been changed by the course and we decided to go our separate ways for a while, though over the next two years we stayed good friends.

It was towards the end of the second year that I noticed another very odd thing happen in my life that I find difficult to explain.

I was living at Mentmore Towers in Buckinghamshire. That was the national headquarters of the Transcendental Meditation organization in the UK.

Dorothea and I had decided to give it another go and I wanted to meet her in Germany. I asked the person in charge at Mentmore for permission to go and visit Dorothea in Germany, but he refused to let me go.

That evening, as I was sitting in group meditation, it was as though all my loneliness and love for Dorothea came to a head. I could not hold this wave of emotion back and I burst into tears. In the split second I burst into tears there was a flash of lightning and a crack of thunder in the sky above Mentmore.

There was no meteorological explanation for this. It was as though the environment were also releasing all the frustration and anger as I was letting go of it at the same time. Even today I feel a connection between what we feel and what is happening in the environment around us, and that it is ever present in our lives.

A few weeks later, after this release of tension within myself, I was sent to Skelmersdale in Lancashire to help set up what was known as the Ideal Village. This was to be a large group of people meditating together in a more normal family setting.

Two days after arriving at Skelmersdale I was sent to pick up a few people at the train station. That was the first time I set eyes on my wife Debbie. I lived in Skelmersdale for eleven years setting up two very successful businesses while at the same time bringing up three really lovable children with Debbie.

After eleven years we decided to buy a farm in the Snowdonia National Park and let our children learn about nature first hand.

In a way I look upon my time on the farm as me doing my "hermit in the hills" bit. The farm was quite isolated and I was free just to be, enjoying nature around me. I learned so much from the animals and found that they even managed to speak to me. You may ask how? That is a very good question. I will give you an example.

As a farmer I would quite often feel inspired to have a look around the farm. I say inspired because I would sense there was a problem. On this one occasion I was being guided into a field I knew to be empty of animals and, that being the case, there had not been a reason to visit for over a month.

The farm was quite large and therefore I had an ATV, which is like a four-wheel-drive motorbike. My dog always found a comfortable spot to sit on behind me. The field in question had high crags and tall bracken, making it very difficult to see more than 10 metres ahead.

I had driven all around the field and was sitting in the middle just listening to the wind in the trees and the sound of running water in the streams. The nagging feeling would not go away! There was something wrong, but what?

I started off to have a last look around, letting the dog off the lead to see if he could help. Immediately the dog's ears pricked up and off he went with me in tow!

As we came over the hill my eyes caught sight of a ewe that had pushed her head through the fence to reach a luscious green blade of grass on the other side, only to get her head stuck in the wire as a result of such frivolousness.

But as I came closer I was given a very big surprise. The ewe had just given birth to a little lamb, which was still alive but unable to get to its feet.

I acted quickly, placing the baby lamb beside its mother to feed, keeping her occupied while freeing the mother's head from the fence.

A few minutes later they both walked off together as though nothing had happened.

But a lot had happened! It was certainly not a coincidence that I was in that field. My intuition took me there just as the mother gave birth to her little lamb. Could it be that the nature spirits were guiding me? Or was the ewe able to send me an SOS by telepathy?

This has happened many times, with the sheep having their heads stuck in the fences. On each occasion I was sent a message. Sheep can only live about three days without food. Therefore somehow they were able to get a message to me, as I found many live sheep in that position, but I never found a dead one.

Which proved to me that the system worked: but what was the system? The system is the field of consciousness we all find ourselves in. Most of the time it helps us to achieve what we want to achieve but now and again it is time for a change.

I found myself amidst a welter of change about five years ago, when the Foot and Mouth Disease restrictions suddenly paralysed the farm. I had 700 mouths to feed, the sheep had to eat! Just 6 months later the farm went under the auctioneer's hammer. How dramatic that was!

The lovely young couple that bought the farm, only heard about it two days before successfully bidding.

Our financial life continued to collapse around our ears. At that time our daughter Lucy was at a Catholic boarding school, which she loved. Debbie could see no way of staying where she was and keeping Lucy at her school, so she moved to Tenerife.

I meant to follow her, but our financial situation became even more complicated and I had to stay behind to salvage it. The upheaval of this time left our family of five neatly peeled of our skin like oranges. Anything to do with financial security had gone. It was a totally fresh start for all five of us.

Thus it was that I found myself with two (rented) homes separated by a huge expanse of ocean. Returning from a trip to Tenerife I wrote this about my experience:

The Day I Saw Myself...

Oh what a day! It started with me flying into Manchester from Tenerife at 5.30 in the morning. It was a nice sunny day, with the birds singing and the wind rustling the leaves of the trees. Instead of going home I had to drive to Machynlleth in mid-Wales, for a court hearing in the aftermath of the sale of the farm.

The hearing was quite emotional for me, as I had to relive that ten-year period recalling that the farm had been much more than just a job for us. I had truly put my heart into it, and our son James had done the same.

The magic of the day started when I went to church that evening.

As always, the love that was in the room at the Bangor Independent Spiritualist Church shone through and had a supportive effect on all present. The medium gave a lovely philosophy talk and had moved on to the section of mediumship.

As always, while the medium was giving messages, I looked within myself with my eyes closed, a little like meditating. I just opened my eyes when he finished each message, in case he might want to come to me next.

The chairman announced to the medium that there was time for one more message. The medium came to me: "You have a lovely energy surrounding you and a quite unique way of coming out of your body and looking back on yourself". I do have the experience of astral travelling a lot and could relate to what he was saying.

He then went on to describe all the angels that were surrounding me and which were guiding me on my path! Again, I could relate to this, as I feel the presence of Spirit around me like cobwebs or angels' wings brushing against my body.

I think he seemed to be referring to an event that had happened the night before while I was in Tenerife. A young couple visited Debbie's house wanting a healing.

The young man, Neil, was suffering from Hepatitis C, leaving him with a failing liver. The doctors only gave him six months to live. When the couple arrived Neil was looking stony faced, as though he were carrying all the problems of his life and the world on his shoulders.

I thought the best way to proceed was to try to relieve some of the tension first before administering him healing. I suggested that we do a visualization meditation, balancing his aura energy that surrounds the physical body.

We began the meditation and, as I usually do, I started by taking the attention inward: first by becoming aware of the feet on the ground, checking for tension in the muscles, then working through the rest of the body relieving tension and relaxing the muscles.

I then made the couple aware of their breathing by noticing the life energy coming in with each in-breath and the stale energy leaving the body with each out-breath.

By this time the silence had descended on the room, leaving it filled with love and light. I brought their attention to this silence and described some of its magnetic qualities. I got them to try to find the boundaries of this silence. Was it only inside the body or did it extend beyond?

I invited them to notice that although this silence is silent, it seems to have liveliness to it, a kind of grain. We played about with this love and light that we all felt deep within our hearts.

I then took their attention back to their feet and started to grow roots out of their feet to connect their energy field to the centre of the Earth. I opened each of the energy centres in the body—the seven chakras—washing the aura thoroughly with each coloured light in turn.

By this time the energies were really starting to develop. I continued to describe my understanding of how the body worked.

I got them to visualize the forever-magical life process. An egg in the mother's womb being fertilized; the zygote dividing again and again, producing many cells from within itself.

As the number of cells increases, seeing them start to specialize in all the various components of the body. Some form the skin, some the bone, some the internal organs of the body.

I then drew an analogy between a piece of paper with iron filings on it and the cells in the body. The iron filings are all random until a magnet is brought underneath. Then the Life Force of the magnet holds all the iron filings in place in a balanced and harmonious way.

In the same way, the Life Force in that growing baby holds and co-ordinates all the cells to grow in a balanced and harmonious way.

It is only the stress of living life that upsets the natural balance of the human system. In the case of Neil he seemed to be carrying more than his fair share of life's burdens with him.

So I got him to forgive all those people that had wronged him in his life. I got him also to forgive himself for all the people he had wronged, and asked him to visualize all that stale energy leaving him, flowing down the roots deep within the Earth.

Again we washed the aura with the light from the chakras, visualizing each energy body being repaired. In this visualization we also included his rents and tears; this light was mending all his wounds.

The energy bodies being left in perfect balance and perfect harmony one inside the other. In this way forming the energy field that holds every cell in the body in perfect harmony and balance, functioning in an effort-less, natural way.

But the real magic of this visualization meditation came when I start-ed to focus in on his physical problem of the liver.

As soon as I mentioned the word "liver" there was such a presence in the room. Every cell of my body started to tingle and I felt that we had some very powerful healing helper come in from the Spirit world to help in this process of healing Neil's liver.

We started the healing in the meditation by thanking all the cells in Neil's body for all the hard work they had done over the years in keeping the body going and maintaining the peace and harmony that exists within him.

We focused down on the liver itself and thanked all the healthy cells for all the extra hard work they were doing to keep the liver functioning. You could almost hear the waves of appreciation received back from them for this loving thought.

With the energy field repaired and with the help of all the healthy cells in Neil's liver, I then asked for all the cells that were not healthy to leave and be replaced with healthy, normal ones. I asked for some of the cells to be sent out as scouts to try to find spare material in the body to carry out the repairs needed.

I then started to close the chakras and continue balancing the energy fields in the body. I slowly got the couple to be aware of their surroundings again and gradually become fully conscious of their physical body and their surroundings.

We then went on to do the physical hands-on healing and channel the universal energy in the normal way.

On the way home from church, I was passing along a particularly lovely wooded stretch of road. It was late evening on a beautiful midsummer's day. The trees and grass looked so full of life energy.

In my mind, I contrasted this with the same scene in winter and realized that what I was looking at, was life itself: the flow of energy, love and light that is the spirit of creation itself.

I then remembered the court hearing and seeing all my possessions of the last ten years leaving me. But these possessions were now unneeded energy like the trees in winter, dormant.

Life is that which is living, that which flows from your heart. That which is in the here and now, life itself, like me driving the car along this wooded road—the flow of energy.

That realization took away the pain of having to say goodbye to my past ten years of life. I was shown what is important, that life energy which flows from the heart, that lets me live my life and experience all whom I meet in the present moment of here and now.

What a realization this was for me: to see the love of creation in all things within me and around me and—in reality—of me too, as there is only one of us in the whole of the universe. Only one Life Force, only one Creator—that which is God itself, experiencing itself in its many diverse ways.

Let love and life flow on. The nice thing about letting go of the farm is that it has let me follow a new direction, using my healing powers and helping other people who have not yet seen the joy of life lived in the moment.

Life is like a living pendulum. We live in a field of opposing forces and our appreciation of this is our experience of life.

We see this field as pairs of opposites: for example, hot and cold, up and down, in and out, happy and sad, good and evil and, last but not least, right and wrong. But usually we experience these opposites in varying degrees, which makes them more like a pendulum swinging on a fulcrum.

We then need to ask, where are WE?

If our awareness is based at the fulcrum, then we experience all that living brings us, as an experience of life from a non-changing and non-moving perspective.

But if our awareness is situated on the swinging end of the pendulum, we see our living and our life as ever changing and the events in life leave deep impressions on the mind.

If we condensed all the swinging of the pendulum throughout a lifetime—or even from the beginning of time to the end of time—into the moment of now, what we would get is a ball of pendulum swinging in all directions around us. This would then look more like a ball of experiences around us.

At this point we can see all of living's choices around us in our life. We see that the path of life did not lead anywhere we could not have chosen to go at any moment. There was no right or wrong path, but just the experience of life itself that we gained by taking that path.

It is the journey that is important and remembering that progress takes place through change. Without change there would be no evolution of the "now" moment; likewise, without change we would soon get bored with the things around us.

Your life is very precious just as it is. Know that God only brings us blessings. Whether events seem positive or negative, they allow us to experience the contrasts that make living life so beautiful. Be your Self in the moment and enjoy the experience.

PART II

The Multi-Dimensional Nature of Being Human

A series of short articles that each brings out a different aspect of being human: these may alter your perspective and bring to light your multi-dimensional nature.

I. Introduction to Meditation

A simple definition of meditation and tips on how to do this at any time

The power of the mind is infinite and its capabilities are universal. Normally our mind is turned outwards, always looking through the senses at the world around us. The senses allow the mind to hear, see, touch, taste and smell.

Through meditation we can turn the mind in on its Self. This process opens up a whole new world to our awareness. By looking within, during deep meditation, we can see all the parts of the body. We can look at each cell, in each part and ask it, if it has any problems or dis-ease within its environment.

This dis-ease can manifest itself as a pain or a growth or an injury. It can be on different levels of the mind or body and, if not brought to one's attention, can develop into a life-threatening condition.

So how do we look within ourselves? The process starts with deep meditation. This is a process of relaxing, normally sitting in a chair or with our back against a wall, which will support our body as our muscles become relaxed.

We can look upon the mind as a lake with the ripples being the thoughts flowing across. A lot of people spend most of their life in this mode, with the senses turned to the world, always wanting to experience and analyse what they understand from information received through the senses.

Through meditation we can take our conscious mind into the unconscious part of the mind and expand our awareness.

This is a bit like diving into the lake: instead of experiencing the ripples on the surface, we experience the water itself. Not only that, we can see the thoughts beginning to develop, like bubbles starting at the source of thought deep within the mind.

This could be visualized as a little air bubble starting at the bottom of the lake. As it rises and the water pressure drops, the bubble gets bigger and goes faster until it breaks through the surface of the subconscious and emerges in our normally conscious mind as a bubble on the surface of the lake, which bursts before our eyes.

Meditating or looking into the mind is a wonderful, relaxing and expanding experience. As you sit in a chair and start to go into the mind, the active mind begins to relax and the consciousness of the mind expands.

Instead of experiencing the thoughts we start to experience the impulses of energy that make up those thoughts.

These can be experienced as grains of light, liveliness in the silence of the mind: a feeling of expansion of consciousness not unlike gazing at a clear sky on a dark night and seeing all the stars twinkling in different magnitudes and colours.

This is a state of bliss consciousness, a feeling of infinite love, of having total knowledge of all life. From this level we can see all the different parts or layers of the mind. We see the Self as infinite, never changing.

This is the "I" that said, "I am me" as a baby. That says, as I grow up to a teenager, that "I" am a teenager; as I grow up to an adult, that "I" am me as an adult. The body has changed at every stage of life, but the "I" within the body has stayed the same. I am the same person I was as a baby.

What benefits people in this busy world is stability. By having the knowledge that the "I", the person within the body, is never-changing and lives on through eternity we gain this stability.

If we bring more of this non-changing state of awareness into the busy life that we lead, it brings us comfort and security, stability in the face of major changes in our life.

Frequently Asked Questions about Meditation:

Q: I find it difficult to stop my mind from wandering.

A: You do not have to stop your mind wandering. Treat the mind like going to watch a movie. As you watch the movie, just let your mind become aware of the white screen the movie is showing on.

In the same way as you become aware of your thoughts, look deeper as though you were looking through them to the stability, the stillness and silence beyond.

Q: I will keep trying to meditate, as I want to master it.

A: Instead of trying, just relax and let go. As tension in your body comes to your awareness, just let your attention be with it. Then invite that area to let go and relax. There is no right or wrong way to meditate; the experience will be different each time.

2. Looking into your Self

An alternative way to look at your body from within and bring about healing and rebalancing

As you are reading this, take a few seconds to look at yourself and reflect. Just become aware of the five senses of hearing, sight, touch, taste and smell.

See the connection with your immediate surroundings through each sense in turn. Feel the connection to the planet Earth beneath your feet.

Feel the Life Force come into your body with each in-breath; sense the beating of your heart, the passage of time from day to night to day again and the flow of the seasons.

You are alive whether you think you are or not. Some people may say that life has passed me by, but life is in every part of you from the beat of your heart to the flow of air in your lungs and so on at each level of your physical body.

Take a second to consider the basic layers that a good general knowledge will tell you exist within you. Become aware of your whole body. Allow your mind and imagination to visualize what it would look like if you could see the organs of the body, the cells that make up the organs and the molecules that make up the cells.

See the atoms that make up the molecules and see the fine particles that make up an atom. See these small particles going into and coming out of the silence of pure Space, like an empty void or a vacuum that also feels full of the potential to create.

At the same time just allow your mind to become aware of the field of energy that surrounds your physical body. And again use your imagination to see the field of energy that surrounds each organ, each cell, each molecule, each atom and each particle.

With your feelings feel the silence that exists in the void, feel the potential and feel the love.

Just allow your imagination to look at one atom in your body and see all the electrons spinning around the nucleus. Change your vision and imagine what it would be like to stand on one electron, looking out into the darkness at all the other positive nuclei radiating energy!

Would it be like standing on Planet Earth gazing up into the sky on a clear night at all the other stars of the universe around you?

As you stood there you might say, I wish I knew if there were any other life in the universe on any of these other electrons, not realising that they are all a part of yourself, and you had just narrowed down your vision to such a small part of your Self that you had lost sight of the whole.

3. Levels of the Mind

A look at the depth of consciousness and how it can be used in everyday life

Most people experience at least three levels of consciousness within their minds: Waking, Sleeping and Dreaming.

But this is a very flat, linear way of looking at the mind. The mind also has depth, as is experienced when transcending in meditation. The mind is a three—or even pluridimensional experience, which is not limited by either time or Space.

Each state of consciousness has its own reality and experiences. If we were dreaming and fell out of an aeroplane only a parachute in the dream state could save us.

In the same way all levels of existence have their corresponding level of consciousness and only by experiencing consciousness on the same level can we hope to have an influence.

Science tells us that consciousness and the movement of thought is an electrical activity that can be measured by an EEG (electroencephalograph). This machine measures the electrical activity in the different parts of the brain. But science also tells us that electrical activity exists at many levels within matter.

The body is a whole being and the mind has the consciousness of the whole, though the body is also made up of organs and these have their own consciousness. The heart functions on an automatic level of consciousness, giving out waves of energy which cause the muscles to contract at regular intervals.

But within the organs there are cells and within the cells there are molecules and within the molecules there are atoms. At each level the electrical activity operates in its own unique way.

At these subtle levels we experience this energy as our feelings, and the electromagnetic field permeates and surrounds each layer in turn, one inside the other.

But what is the common theme in this? It is that on all levels of existence there is order, there is progress and evolution and there is intelligence.

Science also tells us that, at the finest level of physical existence, there is a vacuum state, a field of pure energy without electrical charge: zero-point energy or neutral empty Space.

In this state everything exists in virtual form. This field of pure energy and pure intelligence is the field of Spirit, the unmanifest level of mind and body and the junction point between everything in the universe.

This vacuum state, which is omnipresent, all-pervading, eternal, has been suggested as a scientific way of looking at the nature of God itself.

So how is this order in nature maintained? Out of the void or vacuum comes the first sprouting of energy in the form of radiant electromagnetic waves. These radiate out from every point of creation until they hit something and then the wave turns into a particle and an antiparticle.

These small particles are the building blocks of the atoms. The atom has a nucleus, which is positively charged, and electrons, which are negatively charged. The two types attract each other and the speed of movement keeps them apart, forming an equilibrium. The atom is kept in balance by the existence of opposites.

The cells of the body are controlled by the environment in which they find themselves. These have a more sophisticated method of communication, by the use of various hormones and interaction with the DNA.

The DNA is like the brain of the cell, interacting with the electromagnetic field, giving out information and creating the orderly structures of the various components of the body.

A group of cells in turn form the components of the organs. These again have their own method of ordering the individual parts using the fields of energy or consciousness.

The Life Force or Consciousness creates the strength of this order: if the cells go off doing their own thing, the system starts to break down.

This is the main cause of cancer in our bodies, when cells start to multiply where they shouldn't.

So how do we strengthen this order, to bring more coherence to our body and mind? The easiest way is through meditation and becoming aware of ourselves.

This means, in simple terms, taking our conscious mind deep into our subconscious, experiencing the subtler levels of thought and of our own physical existence. We do this through our feeling and becoming more aware of the subtle levels of feelings at each layer of our existence.

By reaching the source of thought and becoming in tune with our deepest Self, we transcend our physical existence; we become in tune with Space, the universe and all that exists in our environment. We become charged with subtle energy and bring this zero-point, neutral energy to everything that we do.

Our minds are full of intelligence, but it is only when we become aware of the intelligence, that intelligence becomes intelligent. Consciousness needs to fold back on itself.

Therefore self-awareness is the basis of learning, becoming more aware of our body and mind and the intelligence that permeates both. We become intelligent, we gain the ability to use our intellect and make decisions at all the different levels of the mind, body and spirit. When we become aware of our gifts we can start to use them.

Also, other people can experience this same self-awareness that we do. This experience is that of reaching that field of unity. If all the people become in tune with their Selves and work from the same cosmic plan, then problems don't come up.

We experience harmony and balance as we draw through more of this zero-point energy. Synchrony forms between people as the electromagnetic field of consciousness grows stronger and more interconnected.

We experience all knowledge in its virtual form. This is also the meeting point of all the individual minds of the world in a common universal mind. By putting our mind in tune with the universal mind we eliminate the main cause of stress in the world.

When you are in tune with the universal harmonic, you are doing what is most appropriate in that place at that time. You experience a frictionless flow of life which is supported by the environment and all those around you.

As you experience these subtle levels of the mind you begin to realize that it is also intelligent. You can start asking it questions and seeking knowledge. This is another way of gaining knowledge; some people refer to it as intuition, some as general knowledge.

It is also possible to talk to other people at these subtle levels and develop one's powers of telepathy. As with everything in life, you are limited only by your power to conceive and desire what it is that you want to achieve.

4. Increasing Energy in My Body

Increasing energy in the body is like gaining a stronger field of Spirit or magnetic field that brings health and harmony.

I have noticed over the years an increase in energy in my body; this is particularly noticeable around the mouth.

It is like a stream of energy that is constantly flowing almost in a circle. I experience this as a flow of consciousness both within and around my body. On the outside it may feel like fine cobwebs gently stroking my skin.

I look upon this energy as being like a gyroscope dancing on a wire. As long as the gyroscope is turning it is poised and stands on the wire.

This field of energy gives me stability in life, a reference point on which to check the forces of nature that are acting on my body.

It seems to connect up the energy centres of my body, the most active of which are the third eye (in the centre of the forehead) and the crown of the head (centre top). But I feel large quantities of energy flowing throughout my body and also very noticeable in the hands and feet.

This strong field of energy is the force that maintains the order in the body. When the body is relaxed and happy everything flows smoothly and is in harmony.

When my body faces some temporary stress, it responds positively by raising its energy level and being alert for strain or problems, in order to solve them.

This is in contrast to the experience I used to have before learning to meditate. Instead of maintaining a quiet, clear mind, I used to think constantly about the problems which were facing me.

The more I thought about a problem the more agitated I became and the narrower became my grasp of the problem and my ability to find the answer.

There is a clear contrast here: a settled mind which draws from a wide base has a much better chance of solving problems than a shallow, jumpy mind which is constantly reacting to the environment.

Also, one's attitude is important as well. A calm, happy mind that is willing to be helpful and considerate has a much better chance of success than one with a grumpy, aggressive attitude.

This calmness of the body can also be expanded to take in one's environment as well. The people in a society create their own atmosphere. This can be supportive and encourage progress; or it can be negative and life-threatening. Most people live their lives in an atmosphere which is somewhere in between these two extremes.

The point is that we have a choice. We can create a life-supporting atmosphere by our words, thoughts and actions; or we can create stress, which holds back progress and evolution. It depends entirely on us.

In reality most people are not aware they have a choice. They are so caught up in life that they have not had time to think of other ways they could live their lives.

They are caught up in the cycle of action and reaction which is driving their lives. This process is very real and has its basis in acquired habits.

Governments look to education as the best way to raise people's awareness. But this is only half the answer; one needs also to raise the level of consciousness of the individual to bring them more in line with their Selves and the society in which they live.

Improve their self-awareness and they will automatically become better citizens: meditation is the answer.

What is lacking in life and in society is the integration between the various levels of matter, from the finest to the grossest.

This is achieved through meditation, whereby the conscious mind experiences finer and finer states of thought, at the same time experiencing finer and finer states of matter and energy within. These are perceived as a faster vibration in one's awareness.

We create self-knowledge and integration in the various levels of energy which permeate the matter of our body.

Self-knowledge has the effect of increasing our intelligent mind; and the power of integration which we give off to society has the effect of raising group consciousness, thereby improving the atmosphere in which we live.

Most religions of the world share a common philosophy regarding the existence of God and God's energy to integrate everything. But they have not captured people's imagination as to the use of God's energy in today's world. The concept of God as all-pervading, all-knowing, has its basis in our knowledge of today's world.

Raising the consciousness of the knower is needed to integrate and permeate all that exists within the world and ourselves. Today, as our energy field gets stronger and we become conscious of it on many levels within ourselves, we also see the same orderliness in our community and society as a whole.

We create from within ourselves that level of knowledge which brings our awareness of who we are, and God, into an integrated state in our daily lives.

My own feeling is that God, and the vacuum state in Quantum Physics, are one and the same: an underlying field of energy which harmonizes and synchronizes everything in the world; but this system only works if the human mind is fully integrated and fully aware.

In this fully aware state the human mind radiates a magnetic influence which harmonizes and synchronizes not only itself but also the environment around it.

By fully integrated, I mean functioning on all levels and between all levels: a multi-layered mind—which includes our feelings—working for the good of the individual and society at the same time.

5. Healing Energy and the Healing Effect

My understanding of the healing energy which I give out during healing
…is to enliven and channel the subtle layers of energy received from the various parts of the universe and from within myself to the person, animal or planet being healed.

Thus, I understand healing to be like a magnet put under a piece of paper covered with iron filings: when the energy field is strong the iron filings all jump into place and become orderly.

When we give spiritual healing we strengthen and purify the natural spiritual field of energy. This sets the conditions for all the atoms, molecules and cells to jump into the right place and perform their natural function.

When the spirit is strong there is an underlying energy field that holds all the parts of the body together. This energy field can extend to cover group consciousness and the consciousness of the whole world.

This is the energy/spirit or the power of love which guides every part of the body to function naturally.

The way to enliven this energy is through the awareness and meditation. Meditation enlivens these subtle levels of energy and strengthens the whole of life in a harmonious and effortless way.

6. Chakras

A look at the subtle energy centres in the body: what they do, and how to feel this connection. To see the chakras illustrated in colour, please go to http://www.healergeorge.com/guided_meditation_cd.htm and scroll down the page.

Become aware of the subtle energy centres in the body and your connection to Mother Earth beneath your feet.

Reach up to the stars with your feelings and feel the whole universe as a part of yourself.

Using your imagination, visualize each of your energy centres or chakras opening and starting to radiate healing energy from each centre.

Focus on your connection to the planet. Visualize roots of energy growing out of your feet and spiralling down deep into the centre of the Earth.

As this connection gets established, visualize all the negative, stale energy being drawn down these roots. As the stale energy leaves your system, feel an exchange of energy taking place.

Feel fresh, revitalized energy coming up these roots into your body. Feel refreshed, revitalized, full of health, happiness, joy and vitality. Feel at one with the Earth.

Allow your attention to rise up your body to the base of the spine. Visualize your Base Chakra opening its four petals. See a vortex of lovely red energy radiating out. Feel it expanding and swirling all around and permeating through the physical body.

Go through this opening process with each chakra in turn:

The six petals of the Sacral Chakra radiating beautiful Orange light.

The ten petals of the Solar Plexus Chakra radiating a lovely Yellow light, blending together with the Red and Orange, bringing balance and healing as each additional chakra is added.

The twelve petals of the Heart Chakra radiating a soothing Green light. Feel the difference as we move from the lower chakras to the more spiritual ones.

Allow your attention to rest on your Throat Chakra. See the 16 petals opening and a soft Pale Blue light flowing out, mingling and blending.

You can already feel your Brow Chakra bursting with energy as your attention reaches up to it. See the 96 petals of the Brow Chakra opening, bathing you in Purple light.

The Crown Chakra—the Thousand-Petalled Lotus—is your connection to all the planets and stars in the universe. Just feel the universal white light entering through the crown of the head and bathing the whole of your body in the holistic energy.

Feel the auras around your body being healed and repaired by this white light. Allow your awareness to expand and feel at one with the whole universe.

As you bring your awareness back to the Silence, notice the change in tone. Even though we are talking of silence, note that it has a tone, or a ring, or a grain within it. Note that with the chakras open your whole energy frequency seems to have been raised.

Use your imagination to visualize some of your heart's aspirations for yourself and your life. Use all your senses to experience these dreams. You can even run them like a movie over your awareness.

Thinking in the Silence is very powerful, as it moves the whole universe to bring you what you desire. Therefore, dream your dream about positive, life-supporting things, which benefit not only yourself but also those around you. Then just let your dream melt into the Silence again.

As we start to reconnect with our physical body again, become aware of your Crown Chakra and, as we draw in the petals of the Crown Chakra, feel the energy being left in perfect balance.

Take the awareness to the Brow Chakra. As we draw in the petals of the Brow Chakra, just know that this chakra is responsible for the higher mind functions and sixth senses like Telepathy, Déjà Vu, Premonitions, and all the "Clair's": Clairvoyance, Clairaudience, Clairsentience, etc.

As we take our attention down to the Throat Chakra and draw in the petals, just know that this chakra is responsible for our powers of communication. Not just our voice, but also all the senses of hearing, sight, touch, taste and smell: they all communicate through this chakra.

Passing down to our Heart Chakra, draw in the petals and know that this chakra is responsible for our feelings. This is the connection to finer layers of our Self, down through all the organs of the body into the cells, down into the molecules and atoms, right down into the silence of the Void itself.

Now as we come to the Solar Plexus Chakra and draw in the petals, know that this chakra is our emotional centre. Our emotions are stored in the fluids within the body. See the Yellow light of the emotional chakra flowing clearly.

Let's bathe ourselves and the people we know in the divine light of Forgiveness, and as we do so, let's feel the incredible power of this emotion, like a crystal clear waterfall, cleansing and healing everything it touches. Now let's be God for a moment and feel our boundless love for all beings bursting from our heart.

As we take our attention down to our Sacral Chakra, just know this chakra connects us through personal relationships with our family and friends. Know that this web of connections to those we love has been cleansed by the Orange light radiating from the Sacral Chakra.

We find ourselves deep in the Base Chakra. As we draw in the petals, know that this chakra helps to maintain our physical body and our connection to the Earth. See this glowing Red light in perfect balance.

As we draw up the roots from the Earth, we feel our batteries fully recharged by the energy we have drawn into our body. We feel in perfect balance, full of health, happiness, joy and vitality, as we return to our normal everyday level of awareness.

7. Altered State of Consciousness in Preparation for Healing

An experiential guide to altered state of consciousness while preparing to give healing

We gently take the attention within and start to connect to the universal love in our own heart. We start with a simple opening statement of our intent: to connect to the highest energy and enliven this vibration within our own heart.

We ask that we become clear channels for this energy to flow through us and bring healing to the person we are working with.

As we feel this connection opening up we feel a calmness coming over us. Within this calmness we feel the vibration, or liveliness, in the Silence start to become finer, yet more intense.

As our vibration quickens we feel a presence come around us; our aura starts to glow. We feel our body become filled with light and become more fluid and less dense.

We then ask for our guides, our angels, our healing helpers and psychic surgeons to come and join in. As we allow these assistants to come close and shine through us, we feel the subtle changes in our aura. We may experience the feeling of cobwebs around us: a deepening in the energies.

We may feel the power of the presence around us growing. We can feel our connection to the Earth beneath our feet, and we become aware that we are one with the Earth—that our energy field is grounded and connected.

We may feel a connection through the top of our head to all the stars and planets of the universe, and feel at one with everything.

We feel the energy centres in the body becoming more clearly defined as each chakra starts to funnel out and become livelier. We feel our Light Body working on many levels. As the energy continues to increase, our aura starts to expand outwards to contain the higher levels of energy.

Now that we have raised our frequency a little and moved into an altered state of consciousness we are ready to start healing.

As you connect with the person you are working with, allow your awareness to attune to the subtle changes in the energies. During these moments of healing you and the patient share one large aura between you.

You may start to feel areas of discomfort in your own body, reflecting those in the patient. Just become aware of these feelings, as they will guide you to where healing is required on the person.

You feel the flow of love coming out of your hands into the person. Just follow your feelings and move your hands to where they are guided. Always be aware and protective of the person's modesty as you work.

You may notice the energy within yourself increasing further while you are working. On occasions you may feel that you are floating just like a ball of light, or may feel the whole of your ribcage light up and start to glow.

Enjoy the experience and know that love and fear cannot occupy the same space. While you are connected to your heart with pure intentions, only love can flow. Fears—your own or the patient's—will be dispelled and dissolve away in this love.

As you start to come to the end of the healing, lift your hands a little from the body and work in the aura for another minute or two.

Just see the person's energy in perfect balance as it was when they were young and life was flowing in peace and harmony for them. Visualize them in perfect health with radiant joy on their face.

Then slowly move your hands farther away and gently release the connection to the person. Take a few minutes to softly come back to your normal state of consciousness.

Allow yourself a further ten minutes to re-adjust completely, then you can move around as normal. Perhaps during this time we can offer thanks to all our helpers for their assistance.

Just slowly release the connection to the universe. Allow the chakras to normalize; visualize any stale energy being grounded down into the Earth, so your own energies are being left lively and clear.

8. Mantra Meditation and its Effect on the Body

A description of the feelings during mantra meditation

During mantra meditation, I feel that I am creating a self-referral aspect to my existence. Or, put another way, I am becoming conscious of my own existence and therefore changing the intelligence or energy which I am made up of, into a self-referred intelligence, which has the effect of making this intelligence, intelligent.

When intelligence knows itself it can choose to change, adapt and evolve.

I feel like a magnetic field or a gyroscope, i.e. energy turning on itself, which creates its own stability or reference point from which to view the world.

I look upon the mantra as being like a magnet stroking another piece of metal. With each stroke of the magnet, the atoms or parts of the atoms start to line up in the metal and produce another magnet with positive (South Pole) at one end and negative (North Pole) at the other.

Consider using the popular mantra "Aum". If you say this out loud you can feel its resonance throughout your chest and body. It is the quality of this vibration that enlivens one's awareness and expands consciousness.

The vibrational quality of the mantra affects the energy field in the body in a similar way. It creates orderliness in the atoms and I can feel the energy building up within my body as the aura expands.

This energy field is sometimes called charisma or a magnetic personality. I just think of it in terms of having a strong spirit or aligning myself with the universal spirit.

What we are doing is taking randomly placed atoms in our body and making them orderly and lined up—a bit like the difference between a light bulb and a laser beam.

When the human race comes to know its own nature, harmony and peace shall fill the world.

9. My Feelings when Connecting to Source Energy

An overview of the feelings experienced when looking deeply into one's Self

Today I had the realization, for the first time, of total bliss through the night and continuing during meditation. This seemed to come about when I looked deeply into my own mind. By that I mean, turning the attention in on itself and allowing one's awareness to expand.

This flow of energy seems to reverse the natural flow of energy from the source within to the outside world.

When you look within yourself—when you look at the Spirit which you truly are—you see that this Spirit is pure love, pure energy; and when you look back at yourself you create this energy flowing in a circle, and become aware of yourself.

This is the difference between intelligence and intelligentness; this is when consciousness becomes aware of its own existence.

As you become aware you gain self-knowledge, and all experiences in life seem to lose their grip on the mind. I found myself focusing on Self, but at the same time becoming aware of the tension that I had been carrying around in my body.

This tension also seemed to have the feeling of fear associated with it. I brought this tension to my conscious mind and asked the muscles to relax and let the fear go as well.

This process of letting go of one's fears, and merging deeper with the love that flows from the innermost Self, is very healing.

I could feel the love and harmony spreading all over my body as I continued to do this: wholeness and love, the feeling of bliss within and the feeling of separateness from my usual awareness of my physical body.

By this I mean that the awareness of Self-as-Spirit grew stronger, and my awareness of my body and its desires and feelings seemed to become separate.

It was as if, for the first time, I were witnessing the reality: that nothing in the physical world can touch the Spirit essence which we truly are.

When your heart is full with the love and light of Self; when you are truly aware of the Spirit within: its eternal qualities, which give such inner strength; then you become free from attachment to the pleasures of the world. The body does not lose its emotions or feelings; rather it gains inner stability and freedom from bondage.

Your consciousness you envision as pure love and light. As such, any impression on the awareness soon fades in this healing love and light. Their power and strength are full and eternal.

10. Telepathy and the Layers of Consciousness

A closer look at the layers of consciousness and where the power of telepathy comes from

Life is constantly flowing from deep within your heart outwards. You are a spiritual person looking out at the world around you through all your five senses.

Your body is the vehicle that allows you to experience life as a human through your thoughts, words and deeds. Your feelings are what connect you back to yourself.

These layers of energy that surround each layer of your physical existence form your consciousness. Note the depth of consciousness as you drop down the layers of your physical existence.

Then watch your consciousness expand as you drop down into the void, that field of silence like a vacuum that connects the entire universe together. Just know that all the layers of matter come out of this Silence. It is the meeting point between each human, animal, plant and mineral form.

This is the field where consciousness flows when we have the experience of telepathy—a premonition.

It is the field you travel through when you have out-of-body experiences. But in reality you never leave your body; you just move your awareness from one part to another. Just like moving your awareness from your head to your foot.

When you feel at one with the whole universe then your body is the universe and you can move your awareness to any part.

What is the universe around you that you experience through your senses? Well your ears hear the sound waves; your eyes see the frequency of the different colours of light.

When you touch a cold piece of steel it feels cold, when you touch a warm piece it feels warm, but what is the difference?—The level of excitation in the molecules, or the frequency and power of their vibration.

When you smell something you are sensing the vibration of the molecules of that substance floating in the air. When you taste something it is a vibration that you feel. In other words all the senses just tap into a different level of vibration.

You live in a universe of light which is vibration. All matter is just the layers of this light getting grosser and grosser the farther you come away from the Silence within your heart.

But you may say, "It is not just light—I feel love in my heart". What is this love that you feel?

When people fall in love they often talk of the magnetic attraction they feel for their partner.

This light, when it forms into electrons and nuclei, creates polarity of negative and positive. These pairs of opposites then grow into the diversity in the universe as we know it: up/down, left/right, hot/cold, good/bad, yesterday/tomorrow, male/female, and so on.

Electric charge produces electromagnetic fields which we can feel around our body. If we put an EEG (electroencephalograph) on our heads we can measure the electrical charge of our brain waves.

You could say that the field of energy, or magnetic part, makes up our consciousness, and the flow of energy makes up our thought waves.

But understand too that these are on many levels, as I have mentioned earlier.

As well as the energy field around our whole body, there is an energy field around each organ, cell, molecule and atom, which forms an individual level of consciousness, as well as the connection to the universal mind within the Silence of your core energy.

There are also layers of energy/consciousness going the other way. Each family has a layer of consciousness, as does each housing estate, each town, each country—until you get to the whole of Planet Earth.

But astrology teaches us that all the planets of our solar system have an influence on us and our consciousness. These layers keep expanding out to include all the planets and stars in the Milky Way, until you expand out to the universe or the omniverse.

Then the whole of that reality may be just a grain of sand on the beach in another dimension.

II. The Interplay of the Five Elements in Our Lives

A look at how the five elements of Fire, Earth, Air, Water and Life Force or Space operate in our lives. It shows how important it is to keep these in balance to have a happy, healthy life.

As you are sitting here reading this allow your awareness to turn inwards into yourself. We are going to discuss the five elements and see how they interact in our lives.

A good place to start is with a simple example. Just imagine that you are going to do a little gardening. The first thing one does is loosen the soil. By digging the soil what we are doing is breaking the soil up or, should I say, mixing the Air Element with the Earth Element.

The next thing a good gardener will do is plant the seed or introduce the Life Force Element. He will then water the seed or introduce the Water Element.

The gardener has learned that the spring is the best time to plant seeds, as the Sun is getting stronger, or the Fire Element is being introduced to complete the balance of all five elements. As we know from experience at growing plants, if all five elements are in balance the life of the plant grows strong and healthy.

Our life also relies on the balance of the five elements. In humans the Life Force is introduced at the time of conception and, over the first 9 months, the mother's womb provides everything the young human needs to develop. When the baby is born the five elements come into play as the baby takes its first breath.

So it is easy to see the Air Element coming into the body through the breath. The Earth Element comes in from the fruits of the Earth in the form of the food we eat.

The heat of the Sun provides the Fire Element and, to a certain extent, we also have an internal fire in the form of the Digestive Fire.

The Water Element comes into the body by what we drink, and the Life Force Element keeps entering the body by our internal connection to the divine.

As we know, the mix of the five elements varies depending on where we are on the planet. At the North and South Poles the Fire Element is quite weak. On the Equator the Fire Element is quite strong and the Water Element may be lacking, as in the deserts. So our environment may influence the Five Elements within us.

Likewise, with the food we eat, each variety will have one dominant element. For instance the Water Element will dominate a watermelon. The Fire Element will dominate a chilli pepper. Onions may contain a lot of the Air Element. All growing plants contain the Earth Element and the Life Force.

The point of this discussion is to bring to your awareness the interplay of the Five Elements that is in everything we experience, from the changing seasons to the change of balance in the elements within us, as we grow older.

Certain animals have adapted themselves to one of the Elements. Fish from the sea and the rivers use the Water Element. Birds fly through the Air Element. Moles burrow in the Earth Element. Most animals enjoy lying in the Sun, soaking up the Fire Element.

Each day just see how the five elements are working in your life. Do you have a good balance of all five?

Are you taking enough time to go for a walk on the beach and just enjoy the play of the five elements in your life?—The heat of the Sun, the ebb and flow of the waves, the sea breeze on your face. Take time to see and appreciate life itself and its interplay.

◈

12. Multi-Dimensional Aspects of Body, Mind and Consciousness

An overview of the many different aspects of body, mind and consciousness and how they interact with the world around us

If you put an EEG (electroencephalograph) on your head you can measure the electrical activity of the brain. But science teaches us that electricity has two aspects: the flow of energy, and the field that surrounds it. The flow is our thoughts and the field is our consciousness.

In the same way our thoughts have two aspects. Our physical bodies are made of layers of energy and this energy forms a field not unlike magnetism.

This field, which is also a little like static electricity, surrounds our physical body in the form of an aura. There are many layers to the aura, which reflect the finer layers of our physical body.

We think of ourselves as a whole person but, in reality, we are made of lots of individual parts: bones, organs, nerves, skin etc.

But each part is made of cells; the cells are made of molecules; and, in turn, the molecules are made of atoms. These atoms are made of fine particles, which come out of and go back into an underlying field of neutral energy—"potential energy" or "vacuum".

The energy comes out in the form of a wave of light, which flows until it hits something, and then it changes from a wave into a particle and an antiparticle. This is where duality is born: positive and negative, up and down, left and right, and all the other pairs of opposites.

Our consciousness is created from all these layers of energy. The sum total of all the layers forms our conscious mind. The flow of energy within this gives us thoughts. These thoughts again can be on many levels and form links between levels.

But what we mainly experience is that, when we drop down, say, to the cellular level or the molecular level, these thoughts turn more into feelings. It is still consciousness, but we experience it in a different way to thoughts in the mind.

Also, the body is seventy per cent water, and the flow of energy though this is experienced as our emotions.

I hope you are getting a picture of the interconnected nature of the body, mind and consciousness. The physical body is surrounded and permeated by the aura—or electromagnetic field—as described in what follows.

☙

13. Levels of the Aura, Body and Consciousness

A look at the connection between the human aura and the body and consciousness

Become aware of the electromagnetic field that surrounds your body. You can feel this with your hands.

Rub your hands together for about 30 seconds quite quickly so they become warm. Hold your hands about 15 cm/6" apart. Bring them closer together, then move them farther apart. Can you feel the change in the energy as you do this? Do you even feel a little resistance?

This is the energy which I am talking about. To a certain extent it is invisible, though some people can see this aura.

Let's take a look at the levels of the aura and how they relate to the levels of the body and consciousness. A good example that shows this effect is a piece of paper with some iron filings on it.

These are all random until we bring a magnet under the paper, then they all start to line up and follow the lines of force of the magnet. In the same way, the energy field or aura that surrounds the human body is like the magnet and holds all the parts in that layer in place.

If you put an EEG (electroencephalograph) on your scalp you can measure the electrical current of your brain waves. But where there is electricity there is also magnetism, or a field of energy created by the electrical current flowing.

If we say that the flow of energy is our thoughts and the field of energy is our consciousness—and this electromagnetic field extends out around our body to create the aura, we start to get a good understanding of the Human Being.

But it is a little more complex than that. Within the aura there are distinct layers and within the body there are also layers. We are a whole person but we are made of numerous parts.

Take for example the heart: this is operating on an automatic level of consciousness. You could say that it has its own field of energy and the impulses of energy flow through the heart and contract the muscles.

These impulses also create a finer layer of energy, controlling the cells within the heart and forming a finer layer within the aura.

Therefore we can say that distinct layers in the body create the layers in the aura and in consciousness.

Each of the seven layers of the physical body corresponds to a layer of the aura and an area of influence, as follows:

1	Organs	*Etheric Body*	**Physical Blueprint**
2	Fluids	*Emotional Body*	**Emotional Feelings**
3	Cells	*Mental Body*	**Beliefs**
4	Molecules	*Astral Body*	**Relationships**
5	Atoms	*Etheric Temple*	**Group Consciousness**
6	Finer Particles	*Celestial Body*	**Imagination and Intuition**
7	Vacuum State	*Causal Body*	**Telepathy and Divinity**

There are also the energy centres within the body—the chakras—which have an influence on the aura. The seven major chakras are spaced out along the spine and head: Base, Sacral, Solar Plexus, Heart, Throat, Brow and Crown.

You can see from the above how your thoughts and feelings can have an effect on your physical body and aura. There is a need to love your Self, and to do this on the levels I have just mentioned above. Self-love is the best cure for dis-ease.

Choose your mood first. Do not make your mood conditional on what is happening in your life. Choose to be happy, fulfilled and content just as you are. Then you can choose to improve your current situation from a happy, healthy outlook on life by making small adjustments.

You may need to review all sorts of different areas of your life. Do this by being conscious of them and asking whether this situation is currently serving you, or if an alternative would be better. If you feel that there is a better way, change to it. This will help balance your energies and bring you back in tune with your destiny.

14. The Five Senses

A simple look at the five senses and how they are all doing the same thing: sensing vibration

Just take a few seconds to think about the five senses of the human body: Hearing, Sight, Touch, Taste and Smell. You may be aware that they are all sensing the same thing: vibration.

Hearing—your ears hear the sound waves.

Sight—you sense the frequency of the light waves you see.

Touch—when you touch something and it feels cold it just means that the energy within the molecules is vibrating at a lower frequency than the molecules of your body. If you heat up what you are touching by adding more energy—or quickening the vibration—what you touch starts to feel warm.

Taste—there are six qualities to taste: sweet, sour, pungent, bitter, salty and astringent. But these are all just different qualities of vibration in the molecules of the food we put in our mouth.

Smell—your nose is a sensor to measure the vibration of the molecules suspended in the air that we breathe.

Know that each of us is a spiritual angel that is looking out from this physical body; our senses are our physical connection with the field of vibrational energy in which we live.

You may say that there is more to life than just energy and vibration: "What about the love I feel?" Yes, you are right, you are more than your five senses: these are just how you keep in touch with the world around you.

Love is a quality that is quite difficult to define. People sometimes refer to the magnetic attraction between two people, but is not magnetism just a side effect of consciousness?

You could say that our thoughts are the flow of energy as can be measured by an EEG (electroencephalograph); and our consciousness is the field of energy, like that of a magnet. Both love and charisma are quite often referred to in magnetic terms.

15. The Power of Feeling

It is through your feeling and releasing, relaxing and centring your energy that you can truly know who you are. Take a deep breath and stay conscious of your breathing as you reach out with your feeling.

We see all the top scientists, physicists and business people, all using their minds to try to understand life and the world around them. What they find is that the more they look into a subject, the more they realize how little they actually know.

Yet the true process of knowing is not in understanding, it is in being. It is through your feeling and releasing, relaxing and centring your energy that you can truly know who you are. Take a deep breath and stay conscious of your breathing as you reach out with your feeling.

This works best with your eyes closed, using your imagination, creating images with your feelings and expanding your consciousness outwards. You can imagine your energy field connected to the Earth and being as one with the planet.

As you do this, you may realize that your consciousness is merging with that of the planet and you are helping the planet's own consciousness to wake up and become aware of its Self.

You can expand again and feel the connection to the sun and moon and all the planets of our solar system.

Astrologers have known for millennia of this connection and influence. It is time now for us all to wake up and put our energy in tune with Planet Earth and the solar system. Just allow yourself the freedom to dream and feel the connection.

However, we should not limit ourselves by imagining that we are just connected to the solar system. We are part of a much bigger system and we should feel the connection to all the stars and planets in the Milky Way and the whole universe.

Then expand further and feel all the dimensions and the parallel universes and the whole omniverse. There is truly no limit, but the more we feel connected, the more support we will have in our daily lives.

16. Create through the Imagination

I invite you to come on a journey into your imagination to create a positive dream for your life.

I would like to take you on a creative journey into the imagination. Let your awareness settle down and become quiet. Think of your favourite place, where you feel safe and secure. I am going to use the example of a log cabin which I have visited on many occasions.

In your mind's eye start to create the image of this friendly place, which can be an actual log cabin or an imaginary one—it does not matter for this exercise. Use all your senses to create the image: smell the damp woods that surround the log cabin, hear the lapping of the waves on the shore of the lake outside the front door.

Feel the warmth from the wood burning stove and feel your mouth water in anticipation of the appetising meal which is cooking on the stove. See the lovely scene in front of you: a log cabin full of your favourite things, the lake surrounded by forests with snow-capped mountains in the distance.

This is a very peaceful place, a place where you come to create and plan.

Sit down in the rocking chair on the porch and take your awareness within.

Allow your awareness to dream of anything that feels it will bring great joy and happiness to you.

This is a place where everything is possible: there are truly no restrictions; use your powers of visualization to create a picture in your mind of yourself following your dream.

This may be a new dream or one you have had all your life. Give yourself the freedom to dream it now in this safe place; it will be different for each person. This is a very personal creative experience.

Use all your senses and run the creative process, like watching a movie; see yourself in the movie playing the lead role. If you like, close your eyes for a few minutes and watch your dream unfold.

Enjoy the experience and bring in all the resources and friends you need to help you with this project. Experience it on all the levels of your feeling.

If at any time you feel a lack or a feeling of fear, allow your awareness to rest on your breathing and spend a few seconds just being conscious of the breath as it enters and leaves your body.

Know that you can come to this place whenever you like. You can create in perfect freedom without restriction or limitation. Just give yourself the freedom to dream consciously using the imagination and visualization.

Then when you are happy with your creation, allow it to melt into the Silence of this place, release the dream completely and rest in the rocking chair.

After a little while slowly open your eyes and become aware of the log cabin again and the beautiful scene in front of you. Slowly rise out of the rocking chair and start to walk back to the here and now.

Become aware of your normal surroundings and reconnect with your daily activity.

You can return to this place and dream whenever you want just by using your imagination. Have awareness in your daily activity of any opportunities that may come up to help you come closer to realising your dream.

Thank you for coming on this journey with me into the realms of imagination and the creative process of visualization.

17. Reclaim your Power through Forgiveness

A simple way to take personal responsibility for your life and live it from a field of all possibilities: a look at empowering yourself through the concept of forgiveness

Forgiveness is a wonderful gift that we have been given to re-centre our energies within our Selves. For as long as we blame another for our current situation we are dis-empowering ourselves.

Forgiveness is a state of mind: you can choose to forgive someone at any time just by saying the words "I forgive you", and saying the person's name if you know it. Quite often you feel the release as you do this and feel your energy coming back home to yourself.

You can also forgive yourself for all the people you may have wronged or hurt. Self-forgiveness is even more important than forgiving others. This is because we find it difficult to love ourselves if we are blaming ourselves for some event that may have happened in our lives.

This process is all about putting you back in the driving seat of your life—re-centring your energies in the now moment. That means not thinking about the past or future but being aware in this moment, knowing that all possibilities are open to you within this moment.

It is also about being the creator of your life and choosing your mood and direction. If you centre your energies on your heart, and come from the area of love that is within your heart, you will feel the direction to take.

Know also that you are not separate from this world: it is all a part of your Self; and, on some level within you, you know of this connection. Therefore give out what you would like to receive.

18. The Importance of Dreaming

A look at how we use our feeling to dream and create our future

The importance of dreaming is in fact a universal principle to help our life flow freely and without stress. When we dream, deep down in our heart we send messages out to the universe which will structure our future.

Therefore, before you plan your next project, take a few seconds to look inside yourself, deep down in your heart, and see what dreams are there that you have been ignoring or pushing down.

Instead of shunning these, start to look at them with your awareness: start to put your attention on them, and watch your whole future unfold before your very eyes.

This is different to dreaming at night in your head. This is dreaming with your feeling, dreaming with your heart.

It is a very creative process and will in effect align your energies with those of the entire universe: so that every thought, word and action of yours will be in tune with, and find support from, the universe.

This is a process which will help you live a life free from stress and allow your natural abundance to flow out from you in all directions.

Enjoy your power, dream your dream, and create your future consciously.

19. A Vision for the Future

How to work with the New Energy as it enters your body. Feel the change and freedom it brings.

The energies are growing each day and expanding in many different directions and dimensions. During this period it is very important to bathe yourself in your Source Energy. This is the subtlest energy that exists deep within the heart, an oasis that can be tapped just by intention—just by your own vision.

Now that the energies have changed, the way we live our lives has also changed. Be fully in the "now" moment, in awareness, fully alert. This is so wonderful an experience: you bathe in bliss, you bathe in harmony, and you bathe in the pure joy of life itself flowing through you in an eternal continuum.

All that you need is being drawn to you; all your desires are being fulfilled even before you have the chance to think of them.

This is the power of the New Energy: perfect flow of the life energy cascading from your heart through all your layers of feeling, coming out on the surface and radiating from you in the ever-expanding universe.

Bring your passion and creativity to bear on the energy. Give it a direction, a vibration, a flavour: live your heart's dream.

Dream these most profound dreams that you were born with. Dream them—that is, allow your energy to flow with their vibration, with their vision, with love and intent of purpose; and then watch the world change around you as all the energy changes to support your new dream.

This is a very special time, a time when all your dreams can come true. Just let the energy flow.

Start from where you are; start in an easy and effortless way. As the thoughts come into your head, be with them, support them, have confidence in yourself and your life's purpose.

Believe in yourself fully, go with it and see what you have an hour, a week, a year from now. Take down all the boundaries and let the energy flow freely. Allow evolution to flow at maximum speed.

Use the internal guidance system of your feeling; allow the passion to show you the way. You cannot be hurt any more; this is you doing it for you, for your own benefit and success.

You are fully self-sufficient, fully centred in the New Energy. This Self I am talking about, is the coming together of all our energies, combining in a universal soul. We each tap into this energy from our unique perspective, but we combine and co-ordinate all the parts of our oversoul.

All the other people who have joined to our energy for the greater purpose—all the parts—are being co-ordinated synchronously by the oversoul. Have faith, trust yourself and know that we are creating a world flowing with joy. All exist in harmony and peace governed by themselves, by their own heart—free, in love and harmony.

20. The Way Forward into each New Year

As the New Energy comes in, take more time for your Self.

As we start each New Year, we are moving into a New Energy, a new way of thinking about life and living.

Just take a few minutes to reflect on the changes that you have noticed in your life and work over the past few months. There has been a major shift in the energies that form the basis of our thinking and our mind and consciousness.

This shift is one of moving forward and leaving behind the old ideas and ways of interacting, both in the business world and in our personal lives. Whether it is a job you have outgrown, a relationship or lifestyle, just know that change is in the air and is affecting most of us now.

There is a need to be self-sufficient and independent. The changes are moving us from being individuals into being units of a larger, more co-ordinated consciousness.

You may have noticed this in your own life as an increase in synchrony. By this I mean being in the right place at the right time to meet with others and form new relationships or businesses.

There is also a great need to have time to dream and plan things just within the mind or consciousness. This is a move from your intellect more into your feelings, using your intuition and all your creative processes to visualize and let life flow from your own creations.

This may lead to a career change or even a period of not doing anything—just planning and creating with a greater potential for achievement at the end. There is a need to plan on many levels simultaneously. This will just happen; all I am asking is that you let your conscious mind be aware of the process.

Spend more time watching yourself and checking if what you are doing is serving you. Or should you make changes or bring in new ideas? Also, take a little time to see if there is anything which you are finished with in your home surroundings. Spring will soon be here and you can start spring cleaning early this year.

Spend much more time appreciating yourself and looking after yourself. Get plenty of rest, make time to meditate and rebalance your energies.

21. Broadband Connection to the Central Sun

New energy and awareness are coming into our universe and consciousness from the Central Sun.

You may have noticed the expansion of consciousness that has taken place since the Harmonic Concordance on November 8th, 2003. This is due to the new broadband connection that has been created to the universe's Central Sun.

This broadband connection of consciousness is on the level of the crystalline structure of your very being. It is using the full electromagnetic spectrum, which we mainly experience through the chakra centres and in the DNA.

Your feelings and emotions make this connection to these subtle energies which can be found in your heart.

When you transcend the physical body's structure—by that I mean experience the consciousness of your whole body: the organs, cells, molecules, atoms, until finally you drop out into the field of pure consciousness—you transcend time and Space and experience life in its pure form.

When you ground yourself by visualising energy roots going down into the planet, it is possible to take your awareness down these roots and expand your awareness or aura out to feel the whole planet as part of yourself.

You can do this also to take in the solar system, the Milky Way or the whole universe; when your awareness is expanded in this way, everything feels part of your Self.

Also, you do not have to travel anywhere: you just move your awareness around. Just as, within your own human body, you move your awareness from your head to your foot, when expanded you can move your awareness to any part of the universe in an instant just by having the intention to do this.

What are the advantages of the new awareness?
- You notice that synchrony in life increases
- Problem-free living

22. The Universe Within and Without

Expanding awareness of who and what we are: a look at life from a different perspective

As I sit here I can feel the connection through the top of my head to a greater version of who I am.

As I allow my awareness to settle into a meditative state and expand out from my body, it's as though a column of energy or light is coming into my body through the Crown Chakra. As I become aware of this energy and merge my awareness with it, I feel I can travel within the light and expand my awareness out beyond my body.

As I allow this connection to be made, the first thing I connect with is our solar system: our sun and moon, and all the planets that orbit the sun. Many people are aware of the influence of these planets in their lives on a subconscious level.

Many people follow their horoscopes or astrology. But what I am asking you to do with me now is just feel this connection, this flow of energy into your body through the top of your head.

Just feel the energy in an effortless way and then give the intention to have your awareness in this energy. Hear your frequency rise as you connect to this energy.

Then expand your awareness out just with your imagination, so you feel that a ball of your consciousness has expanded and surrounds all these planets, with the sun in the centre. Just experience what it feels like to be aware, on a conscious level of the mind, of your connection to this energy.

Just ask for these energies to come into balance, to flow freely, and to feel whole and complete.

See the many connections between the planets and the sun. See the full range of the electromagnetic spectrum radiating from the sun and the influence it is having. Feel the gravitational influence within the energy and how this affects your feelings and mood.

As you feel this wholeness around you, just innocently allow that energy to merge with your body. Feel the balancing effect it has. Feel the wholeness within, the peace and harmony, the healing effect. Just become aware of the inner Silence and connection.

Now expand your awareness out again and see your connection to the galaxy. See our star and planets merge into a larger plan, into a group of stars and planets; feel the influence of the energy at that level.

Listen again to the Silence, and the tone of the vibration at this expanded level. How does it feel? What is your mood like? Just be the energy, merge your awareness with it. Then finally expand your awareness again and feel that the whole universe is contained within your awareness.

Just expand out to infinity in all directions, in all dimensions, and feel whole and complete. Just feel the energy, notice the Silence ringing and ask yourself, has my vibration changed since I connected with this larger energy field?

Now just imagine that you are within your body, say, living on one electron going around the nucleus of one atom. Just look from that perspective at what you are seeing. You can see the positive nucleus radiating energy: if you like, just like a sun at this level, with all the other electrons looking like other planets.

Expand your awareness out again and see the other atoms that make up a molecule in your body. They seem to form themselves into a kind of miniature galaxy. See all the molecules that form a cell in the body. All these mini galaxies look a little like the Milky Way.

Expand your awareness out again; see all the organs and all the connections within the body; and you see, from that level of one electron looking out, what looks like a whole universe within your own body.

What I am trying to say is that life repeats itself, in layers, one within the other, from the largest to the smallest.

It really is just a question of perspective, and who we choose to be: where we draw the line as to where our body finishes and some other thing starts which is not our body. But I hope I have given you a way of looking at yourself and realising that perhaps there is no barrier where our awareness ends and this other thing starts.

Perhaps, if we were fully aware, expanded our energies out, and felt the reality of being everywhere and everything, whole and complete; we might start to see the bigger picture and the interconnection between everything.

What I am asking you to do is share my vision to expand your awareness out and become conscious of the finer levels of yourself. Realize that perhaps there is no difference and each person, too, is part of everything.

Just look from a different perspective and notice different things about who we are: the wholeness of life and consciousness.

23. Expanding the Awareness of Who and What We Are

Pushing out the boundaries of who we think we are to take in the whole universe

I was sitting quietly last night just thinking this question and a vision came to me. That was, as well as my physical body, it is possible to expand awareness through visualization as to where the boundary really is, of who and what we are.

As I sat and started to look within, in the same way that you can move your awareness from your mind down to your foot, I started to visualize roots growing out of my feet and saw them spiralling down deep into the centre of the Earth.

This was a very natural connection to make and seemed to join my energy field to that of the planet.

I could see the centre of the Earth clearly and it felt a part of me. The main core of the Earth generates the magnetic field of the planet and, you could say, makes its consciousness. My own consciousness seemed to be merging with that of the planet.

As I sat and watched, my awareness started to expand from the centre of the Earth outwards to follow the lines of this magnetic field. The awareness just seemed to expand naturally out from the centre through the fields of magma out to the Earth's crust.

I could see the ley line structure just below the surface within the Earth: a matrix of energy lines showing a structure of consciousness to the planet. The funny thing is, this structure also felt as though it were a part of who I am.

As I carried on expanding my awareness, I took in the air around the planet up to about 3 miles above the surface of the world. This awareness held within it all the weather patterns, including the elements of air and water vapour.

These also felt a part of my awareness. I realized that the weather was the flow of consciousness as well.

The vision I was getting was of this energy field being fragmented. But bringing it to my conscious awareness was having a healing effect on it. All the cracks, all the boundaries started to melt away. A feeling of great warmth and wholeness came over me.

The other feeling I was getting was that, if a number of people held the same vision, this energy field would start to strengthen. Not only that, we would give it awareness and life, and become conscious of another aspect of ourselves.

I could see all the energies coming into balance, not by any external means or conscious effort, but just through this healing process of self-awareness.

I feel that our normal understanding of the physical body, when looked at from the perspective of the five elements, may bring our awareness in line with this understanding of the Earth.

The five elements of: Fire, Earth, Air, Water and the Life Force or Space make up our physical body and also our current consciousness. If we add to that the five elements on a planetary level and bring that to our conscious mind, we have expanded ourselves out to the next level of that which we are.

The planet needs everyone to hold this vision now to become whole. This vision transcends national boundaries and religious and political systems.

We need to connect on this level for us to realize that all the people of the world are our brothers and sisters: no matter what colour, race, or political system, we are all one and linked to the planet.

We give the planet life. So why not do this on a planetary level and also give the planet consciousness and self-awareness?

In the same way that the liver-coloured cells and the artery-coloured cells of our physical body co-operate with the blood-coloured cells, and other organs of the body co-operate with each other to make us whole, no matter what colour our physical skin; the planet also has organs and cells.

You could say that a human being makes one cell of society and each city, town or village has specialized in making an organ of the planet Earth. The roads form the blood vessels carrying the goods and services to each person or cell on a planetary level, just like the bloodstream does within our human body.

You could say that the forests make up the lungs of the planet, producing the oxygen which each human needs to breathe.

The point is, if the planet is going to be healthy, we have to change our perspective of who we think we are.

We need to expand our awareness and see the whole picture and become conscious of it. If we did this, wars would immediately cease, food would be shared evenly, and the other resources of the planet would be more evenly distributed.

Only by reconnecting with our roots and expanding our consciousness can we see the bigger picture. It is up to each one of us to make this connection and to become aware. Consciousness and awareness are the two main human qualities that have brought progress to the world.

Awareness is consciousness knowing itself. Self-awareness is what makes intelligence intelligent. It is consciousness turning back on itself, and knowing that it exists, that makes us intelligent.

All I am asking you to do is take the step to this, the next level of awareness. Expand who you think you are, reconnect with your roots and breathe life into the planet.

24. We are all Human Angels

A look at the relationship between humans and angels

Each one of us is a human angel. We are spiritual beings. The angel within us was never born and can never die. You need to understand who you are! You are an angel looking through this physical body at the world around you.

When you think about it, the Self within has stayed the same even though our body changes its cells every 7 years. Your body has changed shape from a baby, to a toddler, to a teenager, to an adult. Yet the person within has stayed the same.

The vibration which is you is something stable, non-changing. We are very subtle, even finer than the light itself.

We know from physics that the light comes out of the void or vacuum as a vibration: the light comes out until it hits something. Then it changes from a wave to a particle and an antiparticle.

These particles cluster together and form the atoms of our body. These atoms cluster together and form the molecules. These molecules cluster together to form the cells. The cells form our organs and bones etc. All these cluster together to make us up as humans.

But we are subtler than any of our physical body. We are angels; each one of us is a spiritual being first.

Know that you are one with the void, the vacuum that underlies your physical body, and everything in the universe. You could say that you are a part of God, as God is everywhere also.

Know also that this field of potential energy is a non-changing, eternal continuum that has the potential to be anything and is the home of all knowledge.

Think about the Self within the body and just see this non-changing aspect within yourself. Know also that who you are is the silent witness to all that happens in your life. If you identify with your true Self—this non-changing Self—you gain strength and inner stability even in the face of great change.

You are a creative being. You can create out of this Silence within, from this field of all possibilities, the seedbed of creation. Use your powers of imagination and give yourself the freedom to create from within yourself.

25. Calling upon the Angels to Help

Getting assistance from the angels to help find solutions for events in our lives

Angels have been around as long as man. Most religions mention them. But how do we connect with our angel friends and call upon their help?

Most religions say, "ask and you shall receive"; so how do we go about this asking process?

To "ask", take the attention within: you can do this through the process of meditation, or just sitting quietly and letting the mind settle down. When you feel that inner Silence or peace, quietly start to think about the subject you have in mind.

When you are ready, ask for the angels to help to find the solution. Maybe you can start a dialogue with your Higher Self; you may get an answer back straight away.

Or maybe you can call upon the angels to go out and find the solution for you. The angels will then come back with the answer in a few hours or days.

Know that this is a process that takes place within your Self, on the very quiet levels of your awareness and feeling. You can ask for assistance in any area you like. Just use your imagination to reach out with the impulses of your feeling and request the angels' help.

This is a very individual process and there are no hard and fast rules. Know that the whole universe responds to your intentions and will bring to you what you request. All I am asking you to do is try this process out on a conscious level of the mind, where you are consciously choosing what you wish to create.

This process works even better if it will help humanity and the world at the same time. It will work really well if it brings upliftment into the lives of others as well as yourself. Just talk to your angels within and make your request. You will be surprised at how well this system works.

You may even feel the angels going out to carry out your bidding.

Know that as long as your desires are coming from your heart and from love, the angels will support you and work with you with enthusiasm.

You may feel their presence around you when you are working with them. You may feel their wings brushing the skin of your face. This happens most readily with the eyes closed and your attention on your Inner Self.

Always be appreciative of their help and thank them for all their efforts to assist you. I am sure after a few goes you too will feel the love that is generated by this process of working with your angels.

26. Digital Clocks and the Synchrony in Life

A look at how digital clocks show synchrony as the New Energy becomes more integrated

I would like to start with the understanding that all things are within me and I am becoming aware on a daily basis that this is so. I am becoming aware of Spirit around me, and the intelligence that this spiritual energy displays.

For example, my eyes keep being drawn towards digital clocks to check the time. The numbers on the clock usually form an interesting pattern, for instance 13:13—a duplicated number—or 13:31 as a mirror image, 11:11, 22:22, etc.

I have also found that Spirit can multiply. For example, I've had 06:18 (where 18 is three times 6) and 04:21 (where 2 is half of 4 and 1 is half of 2). You may think that this is a coincidence, but it is happening many times a day.

In the car I have two digital clocks with slightly different times, one on the dashboard and the other on the radio, and my attention is drawn to the one with an interesting number for me to look at.

Driving along the road yesterday, after I had gone about a mile from home I got inspired to set the distance counter for the journey, thinking only that I would like to check the mileage to where I was going—about 20 miles away.

Well, just after I got half way there, you can imagine my surprise when I looked at the dashboard and saw the clock at 11:11 and the trip counter at 11.1 miles. I could only admire Spirit for organising this synchrony to happen.

How does Spirit do this?

I have been wondering this myself for the past few days. Quite often Spirit wakes me up in the night to look at the clock. An interesting pattern may appear, for example 5:05 or 6:26, where the two end figures are the same with a different centre figure.

The implications of this are quite interesting. It means that spirits have eyes to see and the intelligence to understand the meaning of the number and which clock has the right numbers.

The question is, is it a Spirit Guide that looks like me with a full body that may coexist in the same space and time as me; or is it the impulses of energy themselves that are intelligent? Like the individual photons of light? Or angels?

This I still have to figure out. I feel both present. I feel the Spirit Guides coexisting with me and in me. I feel the individual grains of energy on many different levels of my body and consciousness. I feel the consciousness of each cell, each molecule, each atom and each photon of light.

I feel the field of energy like an electromagnetic field or aura at each level of my existence. I can move my awareness to each level; I can come out of myself into the field and look back and change my perspective.

What is Spirit trying to tell me?

I am a firm believer that these energy fields connect everything in the universe, that the universal energy is involved on every level and in every decision.

At the same time, I am a firm believer that the mind does have free will.

The field of energy puts forward a suggestion for an idea, maybe on one level of the mind, body or emotions.

But it is the human brain that connects all these levels together and has the knowledge and experience to balance all the levels and make an intelligent decision, or not, depending on what that person decided he wants to create at that moment in time.

When the decision is made the whole of the universal energy rebalances itself and sets the conditions to fulfil that decision. But it is this understanding that each impulse of energy is intelligent and seems to have eyes to see and a brain to understand that I am finding so fascinating.

We all talk about angels—including guardian angels—and invisible helpers. Are these impulses of energy the angels?

Size has nothing to do with it. It is difficult to see the difference between the structures of one atom and that of our solar system.

The atom has a positive electrical charge in the centre and negative electrons circling around.

In the same way we have the sun, which you could say is positively charged as it always radiates energy, and the planets, which are negatively charged as they receive the energy from the sun. The atom and the solar system could be the same, just on a different scale.

27. The Energy of the One

Changing the perspective on how we see the world

The New Energy is making us aware that we are more than our physical body.

The vision I got was of me being just one cell in the body, and seeing the rest of the body from that perspective. That is to say, being an individual cell and yet being aware of the bigger whole that makes up the rest of my body.

It is this bigger picture I would like to talk about. As a cell, we send our energy out and communicate with the body on many levels: electrically through the nerves, chemically through the blood, sensorially through feelings. Each cell must know the whole picture of the body through this communication on many levels.

Now, my vision was that each person is a cell of society. We use the same methods to know the bigger picture. We communicate on many levels and are aware of the whole, whether this awareness comes from a photo of the Earth taken from a space station, or just a feeling on a deep level of our heart or soul.

The point is, it depends on us who we choose to be. Our awareness can be as small as a cell in our body, especially if it is suffering from toothache, or as big as our body as a whole.

With the awareness of the New Energy it is very easy to expand our consciousness and see that our body is just a cell in a bigger scheme of things.

If we expand our awareness to the bigger picture of the community in which we live, or the whole planet; and then if everyone else on the planet also expands their awareness, I can see a new level of awareness and consciousness being created: a bigger understanding of who we truly are as well as being this body.

This is a vision that can change the world. This knowledge will stop wars instantly. The rich will share with the poor automatically as they will see that if just one person is starving, they also (and everyone else) are starving—just like a toothache.

When this energy builds and more and more people expand their awareness of who they truly are, then every cell of society will instantly respond to the needs of another, as happens automatically in our physical bodies now.

This vision will change the whole world and the planet will truly come alive. The speed of progress will be unstoppable as all the negativity in society just falls away.

28. We Are All ONE

Growing co-operation in the world between countries

I am increasingly concerned to hear about the bombing of any country. The governments of the world have to realize that all the countries of the world are important and have their function in the whole development of the planet.

Just as our body is made up of groups of individual cells, which form the organs of the body, so the planet is made up of a group of countries that form the parts of the whole world.

No good can come to the body as a whole, if the cells of the brain decide to bomb the cells of the heart. Each part of the body is needed to perform its own function. Likewise each country can evolve quicker if all the countries in the world co-operate and share.

Only when the world starts to function as a whole and is working towards a common good shall we start to see real progress in the world.

29. A Thought for Our Loved Ones

How to connect with loved ones in the now moment through telepathy

For all those who find that they are separated from their loved ones, I would like to say that they are just a thought away.

Thought is something we take for granted, but it is one of the most important tools we have.

We quite often find that our thoughts are either in the past or the future. When they are in the past we may be re-living memories of the loved ones we are separated from; and when in the future we may be dreaming of the time when we come together again.

But, in reality, our friends and loved ones are only a thought away. We can think of them now, in this moment, in a positive, loving way—without the feeling of loss or separation.

We may have experienced communication with those we love, such as close family members. This communication is using a different sense than our usual five senses of hearing, sight, touch, taste and smell: you could say a sixth sense, of telepathy or thought transfer.

Telepathy uses our feeling and emotions to transfer a message. Distance is no object; nor do we need to know where these loved ones are. All we need is an awareness of them and the loving thought we want to transfer, and to feel this awareness deep in our hearts.

Then, on a deep level of feeling, visualize the thought you want to convey to this loved one. Use all your senses to help in this process. Feel the touch of the person, smell them, hear their voice, see their face, and taste them. Visualize them in your mind's eye in as many ways as you like.

When you feel the connection has been made just, in an effortless way, think of the thought you would like to send them. Imagine their response: the warmth in their heart, the love that flows between the two of you.

Give this love freely from the depth of your heart; give it unconditionally as a free gift. Feel the warmth in your own heart as you give the thought to the other; notice how uplifted you feel in yourself.

By living in the now moment we have all choices open to us. We can create what we want in the moment. We don't need to feel the sorrow of loss or separation, as we do when we try to remember our loved ones from past experiences. Create the feeling you want now.

It does not even matter if they have passed over to the other side of the veil. They are still just a thought away and can send a loving thought back to you in an instant.

30. Our Body is a Hologram of Congealed Living Light

A layman's look into the holographic body of light and matter which we are

We are a part of all that is: our consciousness sprang out of the Silence which is known as the void or vacuum in Quantum Physics.

This first sprouting of consciousness comes out of the Silence as waves, a frequency of light. The photons of light travel till they hit something, then change from a wave to a particle and an antiparticle.

These particles cluster together and start to form the atoms of our body, the positive particles to the centre forming the nucleus and the negative antiparticles forming the electrons.

These groups of atoms cluster together to form our molecules; the molecules cluster to form the cells and DNA. The cells cluster to form the organs and bones etc., and all the parts together form the whole person.

Our body is an interference pattern of light that has changed from a wave to a solid and grown more and more complex as it has built up the layers through evolution and self-knowledge.

Know also that we are a reflection of the whole: that, at the time of our birth, the pattern of the stars was inlaid within us like taking a photograph. That is why astrologers can predict our future from the position of the stars.

This connection also gives us great power, because each part of a hologram reflects the whole. Therefore, when we change a part of ourselves the whole universe has to adjust to reflect the change.

If you take a holographic photograph of a three-dimensional object, cut it up into 100 pieces, and then get a laser and shine it through any one piece, you still see the whole image but each piece will give you a different perspective.

Human consciousness is the same: we all see the whole, but each person is seeing it from a different perspective. Pure Consciousness is shining through us like laser light: shining from the void or vacuum outwards. That is what is creating the ever-expanding universe.

This constant flow of light and consciousness is what maintains our body and what is, in fact, life.

Know that by becoming aware of ourselves at these more subtle levels we can change ourselves just by our intention. If we choose to create from Source, to manifest out of the Silence, then you could say that we become like gods ourselves—or sorcerers or wizards.

Know that this field of Silence, although it is empty, like a vacuum, is full of neutral or potential energy. This field contains all knowledge and is the source of each of our consciousnesses; gifts like telepathy, knowing the future (precognition), etc. work through this field. By changing yourself you change the world and the universe.

31. Thoughts: from Where do they Spring?

Where do our thoughts come from, and what influences produce them?

We experience thoughts coming into our mind all the time, but have you ever stopped to question from where they are coming?—What forces are acting on you to trigger these thoughts?

We have all experienced a constant stream of thoughts flooding into the mind. These normally relate to the issues that crop up during the day. Sometimes we can receive inspiration and start to change something that may make a shift in human consciousness.

There is no easy answer to these questions, as each human is multi-dimensional and also operates on many layers within what we call human consciousness.

I have talked in other sections about the layers of the body and the fact that each of these creates a corresponding layer in the aura, which forms a distinct level of awareness and consciousness.

We experience thoughts on the surface level of our mind as impulses of energy. These have their roots deeper down in our feeling. They may also have their source outside the body: for example, another person, the environment, the stars and the planets.

Thoughts may travel through the ether by telepathy or via mechanical means: by TV, radio, Internet and mobile phone, etc.

It is not important from where the thoughts arise; the important thing to remember is—we always have a choice about what we think. We can think happy, life-supporting thoughts or we can just go with the flow of mass consciousness and accept our karma in the form of thoughts that just come into the mind.

What I am suggesting is that we take a more active role in the think-ing process and choose in the moment what we wish to create.

You may find that negative thoughts have either been projected into the future or originate in the past. If we can stay fully present in the thinking process and be aware and deal mainly with current issues, our thinking can be much more positive and life supporting.

By using the imagination we can choose to change our reality and create a different scenario that may lead to a different outcome. Avoid being a mirror for someone else's negative thoughts; you can be completely surrounded by people thinking negative thoughts and yet choose to have positive ones.

Know that what you create by your thoughts, words and actions comes back to you. Therefore, choose to create a loving, positive outcome that helps not just yourself but those around you as well.

It is always a good idea to follow your Joy in life. The universe uses this feeling of Joy to guide us in the most evolutionary way.

32. Emotions: in What Aspect of our Body do They Operate?

A look at our emotions and how they interact with our consciousness

Our emotions are something that is very fluid and changeable; but have you ever thought what the difference is between our emotions and our consciousness?

Our emotions operate in the liquids within the body. The body is made of 70% liquid and this exists in most parts of the physical body (e.g. blood, lymph, digestive juices, and the fluids inside of the eyes).

Tears in particular are a fluid that expresses a wide range of motions: joy, grief, empathy, tenderness, compassion, love, wonder, awe and reverence.

The emotions are based on the Solar Plexus Chakra and are usually experienced as subtle sensations of pleasure or pain. They are based around the colour yellow, which is the colour of the Solar Plexus Chakra.

Our emotions transcend our physical structure, but can have a major influence on our physical and mental aspects. The emotions also have an effect on our "fight or flight" response.

The phases of the moon can affect our emotions: just as the moon controls the tides and the ebb and flow of the sea, so does the moon affect the fluids in the body.

You may have experienced more wakefulness on the few nights leading up to full moon. The moon radiates the feminine energy; that is why females tend to be more emotional than males.

We can choose our emotions, like our thoughts. It is important to us how we feel. If we feel emotionally happy and content then the body feels healthy and happy. If our emotions are disturbed then it is important to look to understand that disturbance.

We need to take responsibility for our emotions. If we find we are blaming someone else for how we feel then it is necessary to look at that situation and dig deeper till we find the truth.

Put yourself in that person's shoes. Are you absolutely certain they are to blame? The answer may be "no". By finding the truth, you have reclaimed your feelings and emotions.

Take personal responsibility; for as long as we are blaming another without investigating the truth, we are making ourselves feel awful. Through investigation of the truth, and forgiveness if appropriate, we can take personal responsibility for our life and the way we feel.

This is very empowering and gives us the freedom to be fully present in the moment to choose what we would like to do and create. It gives us the power to think from a field of all possibilities, and choose that which brings us most joy and happiness in the moment.

To purify and cleanse the emotions, one can use visualization.

Next time you are having a shower, visualize all the stale emotional energy leaving your system in the water of the shower and going down the plughole. Draw fresh, revitalising energy into your emotions from the fresh water flowing over you.

Say a word of thanks to the water, which always holds itself ready to serve you in this way. The gratitude you express will build up over time and make the process more and more effective.

33. What is Happening in Our Life and Group Consciousness?

A look at how we identify with what is happening in our life; when in fact the same thing is happening to thousands of other people at the same time

As communications become more integrated in our lives, we start to see parallels between ourselves and other people around the world. It is a well known fact that when new ideas come into existence, they tend to appear in two or three parts of the world at the same time, even though the people in question do not talk to each other.

It is as though nature wants to make sure the idea gets out there, so it puts the concept into a number of people's minds at the same time.

That is why the patent system has been invented. Those that can patent the idea first tend to get control, but what also happens is that there are subtle differences between the ideas, so that each one can be developed without conflict.

The truth is that there is only one of us in the universe and it is an illusion that we are all separate.

If we drop down the layers of our physical existence we come to a field of energy that is subtler than our body and underlies all of creation. Our minds all have a common source in this field; this is why ideas once learned by one person become available to all.

I am bringing this concept up now as, when I am doing my healing work, I constantly come across people who are going through similar experiences. There are major changes taking place in group consciousness as we evolve. The pace of change also seems to be accelerating.

What I am asking you to do is take time for yourself to rest and relax; to allow change to happen, as this is how we evolve. Look at all things around you as a part of yourself. "Do unto others as you would have them do unto you" is a famous quotation, but its meaning is more important now than at any time in the past.

Also, be the source of what you would like to receive. This is a time for sharing what we have. We are all one and any pain in the world affects us all.

The opposite is also true. If we can do a few kind acts to help others, these will come back to our Self. They cannot go anywhere else. Share a little of what you have, and between us all we can change the world.

Take time to imagine a perfect world, through visualization. Dream your dream and create lovely positive thoughts in your mind and see the world change around you.

34. My Divine Purpose

Questions and answers on the theme: "My Divine purpose is to help the world to know its Self"

Q. What is the best way to achieve this?

A. The best way is through example.

Q. Can you explain a little more what this means?

A. The way you live your life and interact with the people in the world.

Q. Am I doing the right thing at the moment?

A. Yes, you are one of the leaders of the New Spirituality and, as such, you have to break the mould. This is why you often feel strained and why you need lots of rest.

    The work you are doing is so important and will have a major impact on the world and mankind. I know that I have gone through many changes and I feel the presence of Spirit around me.

Q. Are there ways I can make a better connection to Spirit?

A. Yes, you can be yourself, relax as much as possible and know that you are already doing the most important work you could be doing. I appreciate the work that we are doing together: I understand the importance of feeling connected to Spirit and the universe.

Q. Are there any techniques which I can use to improve this connection?

A. Yes, you could focus more on your feeling and sense the subtle depths of that spiritual connection. By becoming more aware of the Self at these subtle levels you breathe awareness into that level of consciousness and make it available to everyone.

Q. Are other people helping me with this work around the world?

A. You know they are: you feel your connection to them and can speak to them at any time.

Q. Would it help to speak more to them?

A. Silence contains all the speech you need; Silence contains the whole. Speech brings the mind to the point of focus but Silence has the power and the connection.

35. A Dream of the Perfect Partner

Understand the heart when thinking of loving your perfect partner (a dialogue with a questioner)

Your dream is so beautiful and it is never too late to happen. What I would say is, keep your dream close to your heart and visualize fully what it would feel like for your dream to come true and for your perfect partner to step into your life.

Spend a little time now just going back to your dream; remember the rose petals and smell their essence in the air; hear the waves crashing on the beach and feel the sea air on your face.

Visualize your dream partner: see how close to your perfect person they are. Imagine the feeling of holding them in your arms, see their beautiful clothes and smell them. Feel your hearts swell with love for each other. Use your powers of visualization to see them in your mind's eye.

Know that they already exist in this world and are thinking of you in the same way at this moment in time. Feel the warmth of their thoughts surrounding you and embracing you. They are only ever a thought away from you. You're both telepathically linked and will be drawn together.

Be patient, know that when the time is right it will happen and will be even more perfect than you have already imagined.

See the hidden hand of nature working in your life. The trials and tribulations you have experienced have all been necessary. All the pain you have suffered has been put there to temper you, to give you the opposite of who you really are, so that you can have a clear vision of yourself in your magnificence.

Just take a deep breath and breathe yourself in; connect to your higher planes and dance with the angels. Know that God has brought you only angels, so that you can know yourself in this moment of now.

It is time to let your story go, it is time to be fully present in the now moment and to love yourself fully and connect to your magnificence. Breathe in your partner; feel their essence, feel your love flowing to them and theirs returning to you.

Know that this experience is real in this moment. You are truly blessed because you have realized that your happiness is not dependent on anyone else. It is all happening within you, yet it is even more real than life itself.

Know that the process of creation is thought, word and deed. Your dream is the finest state of thought; blended with your imagination and passion, it creates a tremendous power and sets the universe in motion to bring that vision to you in your reality.

The synchrony of life is such that while your dream is burning in your heart, your true soul mate is being drawn to you even as you read this. Feel them coming closer; in every second know that you are together already, there is no separation; your hearts are joined in a bond of love that can never be broken.

36. Be True to your Self when the Winds of Change Blow in Your Life

Thoughts about your intentions and feelings when change comes in your life

It is sometimes necessary to let go and just be in the moment when the winds of change blow in your life. Progress and evolution are made through change; and life would be very boring if it were always the same.

We should welcome change as this opens the doors to new opportunities and allows all our energies to flow in new directions in our life.

When the winds of change blow, stay in the moment and be with your thoughts and feeling. Make conscious choices based on the feelings that will bring you greatest happiness in the moment. Know that your mind draws from a field of all possibilities and the universal energy uses the feeling of Joy as its guiding light.

Stay calm and let the mind settle and relax. Know that you are part of a bigger system and all things are being co-ordinated for the greater good. Use your imagination to plan your future by visualising how you would like to create it. Use positive thoughts and affirmations to declare your intentions.

This is a process of conscious creation and should be embraced with joy, excitement and a willingness to change. When you use your imagination to create you are coming from a field of abundance where everything is possible.

The subtle levels of the mind and consciousness have connections to all aspects of the universe around us. When we create within ourselves in these subtle levels with our mind and consciousness, that which we desire is draw to us in an effortless way.

If you are feeling that a situation is not the most suitable for you, make a conscious choice to look for ways to change the situation by being a little more creative. The stages of creation are thought, then word, then action.

The subtle levels of the mind are the most creative, as they are the closest to Source. The imagination, intuition and the ability to dream are your creative tools. These tools are unlimited in every way, so give yourself the freedom to use them to the full.

37. Energy of the One Mind, Consciousness and Feeling

The multi-dimensional nature of who and what we think we are in this human form

Consciousness flows on many levels and in many directions. There are planes of existence that the human mind can tap into and become aware of the whole plane and its connections. Some of these planes are on just one level, like the group consciousness of the human mind.

We could look at this like the balls on a billiard table. One ball is hit into the pack and all the other balls move to a new equilibrium and await the next thought—the next ball being hit.

Individuals and groups of people move in the same way. The group reacts to the actions and thoughts of the individual just like the balls on the billiard table.

The above example just explains the thinking process on one level. Consciousness is on many levels and planes, and connects us to our surroundings in many ways.

Some levels of consciousness go up and down; some are in flat linear planes and some in spirals and circles. Some radiate out from us in all directions to form a sphere.

We are more than our physical body and our consciousness is part of the whole. We are intimately connected to all that is. We live in a field of energy, and everything in our environment is having an influence on us every second of every day.

The question is: are you a reactor to your environment, like the balls on the billiard table? Or are you the creator? Our mind, consciousness and feeling are registering many influences in every moment. But our mind is also connected to all the millions of possibilities that are out there.

When our mind is present in the moment we can choose what we wish to create. If we are not present, i.e. maybe living in our past or projecting into our future, we may be living in fear.

When we are fully present in the moment and coming from our heart centre we flow our energy from love, which is the opposite of fear. Love is free and creative, and uses our imagination to create a grand future for us. Love is aware of our environment and our thoughts but is not bound by them.

Love can tap into one of the other planes of consciousness and bring in or create an outcome that may not have been thought of before.

Our belief system forms a mask which we look through to see the world. But love allows us to change our mind and our beliefs and, therefore, change the world and our experience of it.

For a few minutes, just reconnect to all your five senses in this moment of now. Express a conscious intention to look clearly through your eyes at what you are seeing.

What you see may be a clear summer's day with mountains and lakes. Or you may see a field of energy with the different frequencies of light giving you the different colours, depending on the vibration of their source.

We may see that the mountains are over there and we are over here; or we may see the field of energy connecting everything together as one, with no separation at all.

We can do this with each of our senses; our hearing hears the sound waves. Our touch feels the vibration of the molecules and atoms through our fingertips. Our sense of smell feels the vibration of the air molecules. Our taste senses the vibration of the food we eat.

I am just asking you to start to be aware of the connection of all things on many planes and levels flowing in different directions. See yourself as a part of the whole, not separate from it. Bring your consciousness into the moment of now and live your life from love.

Choose a purpose for life from your heart. Create the type of world which you would love to live in. Be true to your heart and your feeling and you will experience joy in your life.

Allow your energies to expand and be free. Your heart is connected to an infinite source of energy. Let it flow freely to all who come in contact with you.

There is nothing that you need, only that which you can create for your Self.

38. Free your Self from Past Experiences

This is a time for being fully present in the now and expanding who and what you think you are.

Being fully aware of all your senses and your connection to your environment, take a deep breath and connect to this moment.

Look through your eyes as though you were seeing for the first time. Hear the clarity in the sounds reaching your ears. Do this with all your senses and get clarity on your connection to life and your environment.

There has to be more to life than just this physical connection that is made through our senses. We have all experienced sensations and understandings that we cannot easily explain.

There are many dimensions to the human experience. What we notice is, if we focus on one aspect of ourselves, that aspect grows and becomes dominant. But it is possible to experience all these dimensions at the same time and in total balance and harmony.

The breath is useful for centring our energy; this is a process of letting go. Scan through your body with your feeling; if you feel any tension or discomfort, just take a breath and relax.

This is a time for going beyond the physical, going beyond your intellect. By letting go you can come into a clear understanding of the finer and finer aspects of who you are.

There is no power or control in this state: this is a process of releasing and relaxing and being that connection to your Self. Allow your connection to your Higher Self, life, the universe and God, to flow naturally out of itself.

The qualities of this awareness as you reach out with your feeling are sublime love, peace and harmony. The reason you feel relaxed in this state is that it is a natural experience of aligning your energies with your Higher Self, which is, in effect, the universe and God.

When you have made this connection, if you wish you can choose to have loving, creative thoughts. Using your imagination, your passion and your dreams and desires, you can get clarity on your vision for life and move into alignment with your life's purpose.

As you get closer to your life's purpose, you experience more joy and happiness. Life gets easier and flows in synchrony with love. Life is a frictionless flow of love expressed through your dreams and aspirations. You are life and your body is the vehicle through which this life energy flows to express itself in the world.

The New Energy we are feeling within our Self gives us total freedom of expression to flow our energy in harmony with the universe.

This natural alignment of your Higher Self with your body, mind and spirit into a multi-layered experience of peace and harmony, speeds up enlightenment and personal development.

39. Growing in Awareness of our Body Weight and Dieting in the New Energy

Learning to integrate the different aspects of yourself, so your desires are all pulling in the same direction

I think we have all had the experience in our life, where we choose to change a part of our Self; for example, you may feel overweight and have the wish or desire to lose weight.

This process is mainly about being conscious of our habits and making slight changes which will bring about the desired effect.

Using the example of losing weight, we can work on many different levels. We can:

- Choose to buy only low fat foods;
- Plan to reduce our portion size;
- Drink more water—as, quite often, the request the brain receives is for water, not food;
- Become aware of our feelings around food, and remove boundaries that may cause compulsion to overeat;
- Change our beliefs—of there not being enough food, thereby causing us to hoard a surplus within ourselves;
- Become conscious of our habits.

You may have had the experience of wanting to lose weight and agreeing within yourself to do the above list, and perhaps more as well. Yet, in the moment we are presented with the opportunity to buy or eat, we find we are doing this beyond the desired level.

Then we get all the feelings of guilt and of being over-full and lethargic. If you are having these feelings you have reached the first stage. You are at least conscious of the situation.

By being fully conscious of our feelings and desires and comparing this with our habits and actions, we start to move towards resolution. We can start to adjust our behaviour consciously.

We will always have days when we can do this better than others.

A good place to start is creating your new image of yourself. This is done within your imagination. Your imagination allows you to experience how you would feel with certain qualities in your life. Your dream weight!—Having a healthy diet and living with a lively exercise routine.

Your imagination sets the "blueprint" for the body to grow into; it adjusts the body's energy field and sets your feelings and emotions to a positive support system. Comparing this image and using positive thinking and planning, we can make a real change in our life.

It is all about integrating all the different aspects of yourself, becoming aware of those which are misaligned or not fully conscious or in your control. The change comes in each moment—facing life with this fully aligned knowledge and awareness, to create the desired effect.

40. How does Personal Development Help in Business?

Business is all about work and making money, so why develop the individual who does the work and creates the money?

Teams run most businesses, and teams work best if each member is aligned with the whole group and works in a happy, friendly way. Team building has been very popular over the last ten years or so, but wouldn't it be so much easier if we naturally lived a life in synchrony with our team mates and customers?

Businesses in the past have employed people for the purpose of fulfilling a role and being paid a wage, where the employee may not really enjoy the job they are doing.

As we move into the New Energy and expand our awareness; as the New Spirituality develops and Self-love grows and our appreciation for fellow employees naturally increases, we grow in synchrony and self-realization.

This shift is happening now; employees and business owners are going through major changes, both at work and in their home life. It is getting harder and harder to stay in a job you are not enjoying doing.

Your individual life's purpose and your job are aligning with one another. It is possible to help this process through your imagination, your vision and your dreams, and so to plan the next step on your life's journey.

The best way to achieve this is to shift your focus from what you don't want, to what you would love to have, be and do.

This shift in vision and what you are being will shift your energy to a more positive life, where you are constantly choosing to follow your Joy, and moving into happiness as you take each step in life.

Your job may change during this process, as you become more aligned with your life's purpose and your employer's expectation. Companies are living things and they can only grow through change as they evolve and expand.

Employees also like changing and growing, both within the company and within their own life. So what can we do to speed up this process of evolution and growth?

Turning the attention back on your Self is one of the most useful things that you can do. This can happen as easily as becoming aware of your own breathing; reaching out with your feeling; adjusting your energies each time you become aware of some tension within the body, relaxing and re-centring.

Following one of the many methods of meditation can do it; the main thing is, we look within and just observe what we feel and see.

We cannot use our gifts until we become aware of them. Taking a few minutes each day to align our own energies will have a tremendous effect on our co-workers and bring harmony and peace into the workplace.

41. Debt and the New Spirituality

How do we look at debt in the New Energy, and how can we bring balance into our lives again?

Overcoming the stigma of being in debt, growing in self-confidence, and regaining one's own centre and equilibrium again, is easy in the New Energy. This is all about being true to yourself: what we have been doing in the past is buying into other people's beliefs and concepts.

In the New Energy the Self is strong, and we realize that no-one can make us feel bad and down unless we buy into that idea ourselves. All possibilities are open to us in every minute of every day. We choose what to allow our mind to dwell on. If you are not enjoying what you are thinking—change your mind about it.

Stop thinking about what you don't want—your fears and dreads—and start to imagine what you do want; focus on what brings you pleasure and joy. The universe's guiding system is to step into Joy and happiness in each step on the path of evolution.

Remember that recovering the money from the debt is the lender's problem. The reason you may have got into debt is that you were doing a job you do not enjoy. Think clearly what your life's purpose is, what you came to this planet to achieve during this lifetime.

Is what you are doing taking you towards that goal? If not, choose again and, as you step back into your life's purpose, see the abundance flow in. Feel the joy and happiness expand and all your problems melt away.

Remember, the world is as you are: if you are feeling strained and tense, there is strain and tension in all you do. If you are feeling relaxed and happy, these qualities spread all around you.

This is a process of letting go. Let go of your past, release your fears and start to dream and imagine what you want. Focus on what would be perfect for you at this moment; focus on that which brings you feelings of joy and happiness.

Feel the abundance come around you and support you as soon as you change how you are feeling. Look for things you can praise and appreciate in nature and the joy of just being alive.

Release your Self from the bondage of money. Just take a banknote out of your pocket and find someone who has less than you; express your abundance in that moment of giving, then see your life change.

Release the hold money has over you; look for ways you can just be of service to others and mankind. Know that money has no value except the value we give to it, with our thoughts and beliefs.

Release that energy back into the universe and see how you feel. Sense the strands of bondage dropping away as you grow in awareness of your own inner source of abundance.

Start to smile again and radiate joy wherever you go. Share what you have within you with all around you. Give from your heart and express freely that love you have within your soul. Then watch your life change and all the abundance flow back to you.

42. How to Breathe Health into your Body through Conscious Breathing

A look at how the breath can be used to bring balance into areas of our body and mind

The breath is very powerful; it has been used for centuries by yogis to create different effects on the body and mind.

Before we start to discuss the different techniques which can be used to balance the body, let's look at normal breathing. It is good from time to time to make sure that you are using the full capacity of your lungs when breathing.

Let's take a few deep breaths, breathing in through the nose with the mouth closed, if this is possible for you to do comfortably. It is important to breathe deeply right down into the abdomen and then to fill the chest.

It is also important to breathe out fully, using the diaphragm to empty your lungs completely as, unless you get most of the stale air out, you cannot breathe in fresh air.

Even using just normal breathing like this, and staying conscious of the breath as it enters and leaves the body, can be very powerful.

To heal any area of the body, stay conscious of the breath, and take your awareness to the dis-eased area; spend a few minutes with your awareness in that area, being conscious of the feelings and emotions which come up. Keep being conscious of the breath as you breathe.

The breath uses air, one of the five elements, to connect with your Source Energy. The Source Energy comes into your body through the breath. It is sometimes referred to as prana or chi.

When you stay conscious of your breath while breathing you get control over this Life Force, and can direct it, using your awareness, to different parts of the body to bring healing and balance into that region.

Even spending just a few minutes a day doing this type of conscious breathing can make major changes in the health of your body and mind.

When major events happen in your life it is quite often a good idea to take a few deep breaths before you choose how you would like to react to that situation. It gives you time to think, quietens the mind and connects you to Source Energy, so that your reaction is coming from love and from your heart.

43. I am a Part of the Universal Life Force

Speaking in public is challenging for a number of people.
Public speaking is said to be one of the biggest challenges in many people's lives. This is all about perspective and who we think we are.

If we think that we are this human body and all out there are different from us, and separate, then this leaves a gap through which fear can creep in.

If we think that we are a part of the Universal Life Force that shines through all of life, we become aware that our body is just one aspect of a greater whole and we are part of that whole and included in it.

This universal energy that is shining through us and gives rise to our thoughts and feelings is pure love: so what is there to fear?

Should we fear ourselves?

If we see all of the human species as a part of the Universal Life Force, and we see this force as the source of our own consciousness and awareness, then the true reality is that when we speak to others we are just speaking to different aspects of our Self.

There is no separation: there is only communication within the body of the society in which we live.

Just as our eyes communicate with our brain, each cell of our body speaks to each other cell. We are the cells of society and when we talk to others we are just communicating the information to another aspect of our Self on a higher level.

Therefore, have confidence in the system and know that when you get up to speak, the group consciousness in the room will draw out of you that knowledge which will most benefit the group. You are just the channel which the information is flowing through.

It is always best to be fully present in the moment and be sensitive to your feelings. It is sensible to prepare your material for your speech, but it is best not to read this prepared material, rather to be sensitive to the energy in the room.

Just have main points that you would like to get over and allow the "moment of now" to assemble your ideas and talk through you.

You are much more than your physical body and by being relaxed with an expanded awareness you will feel the guidance of your Higher Self as you present your talk.

44. Child Abused and its Effect on the Emotions

Understanding how to overcome the negative thoughts around child abuse by a family member; how to re-centre your energies in the now moment

Child abuse is much more common than is usually expressed in public.

I recently attended an event where people were asked to discuss their darkest secrets. Out of the thirty or so women in the room, nearly two thirds expressed their darkest secret as being about child abuse. Two had had an abortion after becoming pregnant by a family member.

The effects on the emotions and on relationships can last for many years afterwards.

Because we often love the family member, we end up with mixed emotions regarding the incident.

As time goes by, these events settle down into our subconscious and only resurface when certain trigger points are pressed. This may happen when we start to become intimate with a person we like.

If this has happened to you I feel the time is right now for you to allow these feelings to come back to the surface of your mind so you can start to resolve the issues around sexual abuse.

We cannot change our past or what has happened in our life. We also cannot change other people; we can only really work on ourselves and our reaction to what has happened in our life.

What I would first suggest you do is embrace the dark side of your life and the events that have happened. Come from the heart and be fully present in the now. The moment of now is all that exists: the past is just a memory, and the future has not yet manifested.

If you find that you have repetitive thought patterns in your life that make you sad—change your mind about them. In the now moment, when you find one of these repetitive thoughts coming up, change your mind.

It may be a belief you hold that was given to you by your parents. Question that belief now and see if it is still serving you.

When you are in the now moment all possibilities are open to your thinking; you can make life up however you like. Just as an experiment, bring to mind one thought about your childhood that has been troubling you for years.

Look at it closely and see what belief you are applying to that situation and what judgement you have made. Do you know for certain that these thoughts are true? Or may you be coming from False Evidence Appearing Real—FEAR?

Fear can only exist when we are remembering the past or projecting into the future; it cannot exist in the now moment. Why?—Because in the now moment we are coming from love; our thoughts and feelings are coming from our heart and radiating outwards, and our heart is full of love.

Fear and love are two opposites that cannot occupy the same space.

So when the past comes to haunt you, look it straight in the face and ask yourself how you want to react to this memory.

Check if your reaction is coming from love, from your heart. Ask yourself in the moment, what would I love to create and believe, in place of the past beliefs and understandings that are no longer real for me?

In that moment, embrace it all, love it all and choose a positive, constructive outcome that will serve you and those around you. Release the past and let the stale, negative energy be grounded into the Earth beneath your feet.

Move forward to the grandest, greatest vision of who you desire to be and step into that. Hold your head up high knowing that you have faced your deepest fear and proved to yourself that it had no substance to it.

Use your mind to dream a bright new future for yourself. Give yourself a pat on the back and love yourself for who you are now in this moment. Overflowing with love and gratitude to yourself, embrace that vision of who you are today. Start to take care of yourself in new ways.

I honour you.

45. Raise Your Feeling Frequency with a Loving Smile

Life is to be lived in joy and happiness. If you are not feeling joy in this moment, think again!

In every moment of our life we have the choice to think any thought we like. Sometimes we forget that we have the freedom to choose what we think in any moment. It does not matter what is happening in our life and what we are surrounded by.

We can choose to change our vibration and feel happier, just by our intention. If your current thoughts are heavy and feel like they are holding you down, choose to change your mind on what you feel. Smiling softly and lovingly will start to raise your frequency and heighten your loving feeling for yourself and others.

Know that your thoughts have attractivity, and similar thoughts will be drawn to you. Feel 100% happy in each moment just by choosing to.

Raise your frequency with positive, loving thoughts of things you can appreciate with joy; imagine these things being drawn into your life.

You are a creative being; allow yourself to think your highest thought.

Dream your sweetest dream, feel your frequency rise, lightening and starting to glow like a magnet; feel the energy of love coming around you. Feel the power of your Self-love and appreciation. Use your breath to connect to your finer feeling levels by consciously breathing.

Breathe and feel the love coming in with each breath. Feel your energies expanding and gaining in presence and charisma. As you become in tune and connect with your Higher Self, feel yourself becoming as one with the universe.

Feel the connection to what you desire, feel it as a part of yourself with no separation.

Know that you have what you desire within you already. Your dream is fulfilled as soon as you dream it. The object you desire is already available to you in your imagination. Know that the imagination is the finest level of the creation process.

Your energies start to glow and vibrate with these high frequencies and your love becomes more subtle and refined. Know that these finer feeling levels connect you to your universal energy.

Ask your guides and helpers and angels to come around you. Give yourself permission to talk with these subtle friends. Ask for help with the issues in your life. Know that these issues are caused by an imbalance in the energies.

By loving yourself and connecting to your Higher Self and finer levels of feeling, know that you are automatically balancing the energies around you.

There is no effort involved with this process. As your joy and love increase, so your life will start to flow in a frictionless way. Just watch your Self grow in all these loving qualities that you have chosen to focus on with your feelings and your thoughts.

Grow in peace and happiness by conscious creation and by raising the loving feelings, and watch your life flow with these qualities.

46. Turn up your Energy Levels and Start to Radiate your Divine Love

Now is the time when the energy of consciousness is starting to glow and radiate all around us. We increase our energy levels through self-awareness.

In the spring of 2005, I attended the Seeds of Transformation Conference in New York State, where I demonstrated how to increase energy and charisma through divine connection in deep meditation. The conference was organized by the Humanity's Team and held at Bard College.

The conference was describing the Seeds of Transformation, where each human is becoming the source of their own radiant being.

By taking your awareness within and altering your beliefs and your understanding of who and what you are, you can choose to start to glow and radiate. You can feel this field of energy all around you without any effort as we move into this Age of New Spirituality.

Know that, as this energy increases around and within you; as you become more self-aware; your radiance and divinity start to glow from within. Your natural beauty is shining from within as all the cells, molecules and atoms in your body become more coherent within this energy.

All stress in your life is starting to drop away, as you let go of your attachment to your environment and the things in your life. Your thoughts and feelings naturally become in tune with the universe and nature.

Start to become consciously aware of your breathing; feel the Life Force entering your body as you breathe. Use your imagination to create your dream and realize your passion; follow your heart's desire to realize your true nature.

Know that your Higher Self is connected to the whole universe. Take your awareness within, connect with that Higher Self, and use your feeling and your passion to guide you.

Fill yourself with your own Self-love; use your awareness to know yourself and appreciate that you are one with everything.

Recreate your Self anew in the moment of now. There is no limit to this process except the limits you set for yourself. Expand these limits and change your beliefs so that you feel comfortable with your Self.

Be happy by yourself; this is a time for self-sufficiency. Make up each day anew. Change your routine each day; flow your energy in new ways. Change your mind about things which bring you pain. Change your beliefs and your judgements about things in your life. Alter your perspective.

Let synchrony into your life. Feel the whole of your environment coming in tune with you. See the things you desire in your life flowing to you naturally. Open out your boundaries and flow your energy freely; see that everything you need is already there.

Your desires are fulfilled before the need arises; see synchrony bringing you all you could ever want in an effortless way. Use the angels to give wings to your dreams. Ask the angels to help you expand who you are and your influence in the universe.

Be that which you wish to create in the world naturally; go within yourself and create in your heart the dreams which you would like to see in your environment. Let go of the old and create the new with joy and fulfilment.

Progress is made through change; start to be the source of your own change.

This process will help to balance the energies in the world. Communication is now so fast that goods and services can be moved around the planet; wherever there is a need, another part of the globe will have the goods to fulfil that need.

Be part of the change and start by changing yourself from within.

47. Working with Crystals to Help with Healing and Connecting

Crystals are like tuning forks: they bring in a specific frequency and can be used to bring your body's energies into balance.

It has been known for thousands of years that crystals and gemstones can have an influence on your body, mind and spirit. Crystals and gems have connections to your astrological chart and there are books and tables available in most crystal shops to show these links and influences.

Quite often people tell me that their favourite crystal or gem found them—meaning that they felt drawn or physically attracted to a specific type and one specific stone. This is tied in with the synchrony in life: that which we resonate most closely with is drawn to us.

I have noticed myself that when I choose a crystal to hold while meditating, I feel the frequency of that crystal travelling up my arms and permeating all of my being. This is a combination of crystal structure and vibration.

There is a need to be relaxed and open when choosing a crystal to work with. Use your intention to help you choose the influence you desire the crystal to have. The quality you desire will be drawn to you and you will find yourself selecting a crystal with that quality.

We are all creating our lives in the moment and your intention and desire are more important than the crystal you select.

It is important to put yourself first in this process. Your feelings and emotions should be your guiding light. Your rational mind and the look and physical qualities of the crystal should take second place, as your internal feeling and the internal qualities of the crystal are much more important.

When you have selected a crystal that feels right for you, hold it in meditation and ask to be allowed to work with it.

As you go deeper in meditation, feel the connection at a cellular level, at a molecular level and at an atomic level within yourself and the crystal. Feel the crystal's structure and the influence it has on your body, mind and spirit.

Become aware of the balance within the crystal of the five elements of fire, earth, air, water and the Life Force or Space. Reach out with your feelings and feel the influence of the stars and planets on the crystal and which astrological sign is most dominant.

Then, when you have allowed your awareness to connect on all these levels, let go and transcend them all. Become one with the crystal and become one with yourself.

On this level of being, just feel what it is like to be one with the crystal. Be in the crystalline matrix, feel its boundaries and influences; then transcend again into a deeper level of being, where all the boundaries melt away and you feel fully expanded and at one with the whole universe.

Know that, as this process of letting go and expanding your awareness takes place, your energies are naturally being rebalanced and put in tune with the whole universe.

Know that, when you come out of meditation, your life will experience more synchrony, and a feeling of connection and support will be dominant in your awareness.

You are truly blessed when you come to know yourself from within.

48. Earth as Our Body

What does it mean to look at the Earth as you would your own body?

We hear it said that the rain forests are the lungs of the planet, oxygenating the air that we breathe.

Our body is made of about 70% water and the planet's surface is covered with about the same area as water. The weather mainly involves the movement of water or water vapour.

Our body emotions flow through the water in our body and often come to the surface as expressions of emotions through tears in our eyes; while with the weather we may talk of an angry storm or a chill wind. When we are feeling a little depressed we may talk of the dark clouds hanging over us.

The different countries can take on the different qualities of our body. For example, the skin colour of the people in each country differs.

Many of the people of Africa and the Caribbean have a skin colour resembling the colour of our liver and kidneys. Our blood is red, our bile is yellow, and the pupils of our eyes are black, till we can find an example of all the colours of all the races in the world within the cell colours of our own body.

What I am portraying here is a comparison which really makes you think.

If the people of the world are really the same as the cells of the body on a conscious world level, we need to look at the world in a whole new way. For one country to wage war on another is like the brain attacking the heart.

What you end up with is heart dis-ease. The same on the planet—war between countries only hurts the world and should now be treated like a disease or illness. If there were a war going on in our body and there were dis-ease, we would become aware of this with the feeling of pain.

It would be described, for example, as liver failure, as the cells would have died due to constant bombardment of the immune system or too much work or pollution within the body. The same with the planet; we have to respect the wholeness and oneness of life on our planet.

If we find conflict in the world, treat it with love not war. War destroys the organs of the living world like liver or heart dis-ease; while love is like healing, bringing new growth, balance and health to the diseased area.

We are now moving into the New Earth—a time when we see and

experience the wholeness of life. Let's all start to breathe love into areas of conflict and bring healing both to ourselves and the planet on which we live.

As we learn to calm our feelings and emotions we will see the weather patterns coming back into balance. Let's learn to love and respect all life and see it as a part of ourselves.

49. Unexplained Psychic and Spiritual Experiences

I feel at some time in the life of each of us, things happen to us which cannot be explained. We feel a hidden power was at work.

I think the first experience I can remember was when I was working for the TM (Transcendental Meditation) movement in Switzerland and had just been cleaning a corridor outside the Maharishi's bedroom. As I was passing the door a pandit came out who wanted to use the vacuum cleaner to clean the room.

I gave him the machine and waited outside. After a few minutes I noticed that he had finished using the machine and it was just inside the door.

Not thinking, I stepped forward to remove the vacuum cleaner. As I crossed the threshold I was zapped by an unseen energy field, like static electricity, which seemed to short-circuit all my nervous system.

For the next twenty minutes or so, I had to sit on a chair in the corridor to re-centre my energies. For a few hours afterwards, I kept having dizzy spells. To this day, I am not quite sure what zapped me but I know that something unexplained happened to me.

A few weeks later I heard of the practice of building a "protective kavach or shield" to protect your property; I am not sure if it was one of these I short-circuited, or just a very strong presence from a highly developed being.

Another thing I noticed was that street lights would often go out as I was walking under them. This had been happening for a few months and I had been mentioning it to some of my friends.

On this particular day I went to church in a car with two of my friends. On the way back we came over a flyover and the person driving said, did you see that? So I asked him, see what? He said, the street light just went out. I told him not to worry as this happens all the time to me.

Anyway, the next minute, the driver stops the car. I ask why he is stopping and he says, another one has just gone off. By this time he is sounding a bit anxious. We set off again, and a third streetlight goes off as we drive under it. I must admit this was the first time I got three in a row.

About six months later I was visiting my family who live in Tenerife and had just told the story to a couple of people in the room. One of the girls said, well, make that street light over there go out, pointing to it.

I told her, it doesn't work like that; anyway, a few minutes later I noticed it was getting dark in the room and walked over to switch the ceiling light on.

The next minute there was a big flash and a bang and the lights fused. For months afterwards no-one could get that light to work again!

50. Our Angels and Guides Helping to Protect Us

An example of where I have received help from my Angels and Guides

The first example that comes to mind happened a number of years ago. I was driving the car down to the South Coast of England to visit my wife's parents with my wife and our three children in the car.

We had been driving for about three hours and were just going around London on the M25. As we were going up a hill, I was in the fast lane going at the speed limit. Just before we reached the crest of the hill, I got this urgent message in my head that said: Stop.

I immediately started to slow down, not knowing why! As the car went over the crest of the hill there was standing traffic in all lanes, as there must have been an accident. I tried to brake harder but realized I was not going to stop in time.

Anyway instead of braking to the point of skidding, I was guided to a gap between the fast lane of traffic and the crash barrier. I still passed three cars in this narrow gap before I was able to bring the car to a standstill.

If I had not had that message from my guardian angel before I came over the top of the hill, I would have been going too fast to be able to control the car. In the end the only damage the car received was an inch-long scratch along the side from a reflector fixed to the crash barrier.

51. Being Present and Alert: What Does This Mean?

What are the advantages in our life of being present and alert? Why is it important to have these qualities in our life, and what does it feel like?—Often people say it is not what you are doing that is important; it is what you are being.

Being awake and alert is something we take for granted as our natural state of consciousness.

There are many advantages to becoming conscious of this state of being, for a few minutes each day. Being conscious of that inner state of being, feeling the presence of the electromagnetic field that permeates our physical body and forms the aura around it is very important.

By becoming aware and conscious of this field of energy, we set up feedback loops which help to increase its presence and strengthen the flow.

So what does it feel like to be present?

After reading this, try closing your eyes. Allow your awareness to settle, and relax. Look within yourself and, using your feelings, see if you can sense the energy flow within your body. See if you can feel or become aware of the presence of the aura around the body.

You may feel this in many different ways.

As you look deeply within yourself you may feel the inner bliss, the liveliness within the Silence. As you smile you may feel the energies flow in a different way around your face and body. As you become conscious of your breathing, you may feel the Life Force coming in with each in-breath.

You may become conscious of the various flows of energy around your body: the flow which causes your lungs to expand and contract; the flow which pulses to create your heartbeat.

You may become aware that strong thoughts sometimes cause a physical sensation or pulsing in the flesh somewhere.

There are many ways to become self-aware. It is more the process of self-awareness that is important: the turning of consciousness back on itself to gain Self-knowledge.

All things in the universe display intelligence and have orderliness within them. But it takes the human mind to turn this intelligence back on itself—to convert this intelligence into intelligentness, by becoming Self-aware.

By becoming self-aware we become intelligent and can make choices.

Also, it is only when we become aware of our gifts that we can start to use them.

As you get good at this process of self-awareness, you may begin to become aware of the matrix that makes up your flesh and bones.

Sense the layer formed by each field of energy at the level of the organs, cells, molecules and atoms of your body and their associated levels of awareness.

You may transcend matter altogether and become aware of the light body that interacts with the zero-point energy of Space itself, which permeates all things.

You may realize that you are this Space, the Life Force itself, and not the physical body at all. You are the eternal continuum of life, which is unmanifest and non-changing: the silent witness to all that happens in your existence.

You may choose to take the awareness out of the physical body altogether and go astral travelling around the universe, flowing into and out of the various dimensions.

You may realize that you can look through the eyes of an insect on a wall in a far distant land and do remote viewing. You may choose to become conscious of what is in the next room and effectively just walk through the wall with your awareness.

When your awareness is within the quantum field of Space, the zero-point energy or neutral energy, you have total freedom. This is a field of all possibilities and you are limited only by your own creativity and imagination. You have become aware of yourself and mastered yourself.

52. Being your Self in Life

Being your Self in life is all about bringing out those qualities that make you unique and different from those around you.

Create the time, for a few minutes each day, to look within and allow your imagination and psychic powers to commune with your Higher Self—that connection to the whole universe around you—to look for guidance and inspiration on your life's journey.

Bring your energies back in tune with your Self and allow your music to flow though you. This is all about living in harmony with yourself and the environment in which you reside.

Use your feelings to reach out and sense that which will bring you joy and pleasure, and use these experiences of life to guide you on your path, your journey into the unknown.

Be prepared to take that further step into the unknown: life begins at the edge of your comfort zone. This is all about expanding what and who you wish to be in the world.

Be prepared to stand by yourself being different to everyone else. You are unique; allow these unique qualities to shine through. At every step of life there is a choice to make; there are many paths to walk.

Know that you are making up your path; you are creating and walking it with each step you take. Do not wait to take the next step otherwise the whole universe will wait with you.

Be bold and have faith; you cannot get it wrong. Life is flowing through you; you are the expression of Life in action. There is no separation, only the infinite flow of love expressed through you in your every step on the journey of life.

53. Can you Help me to Find out why I've had so Many Health Problems?

I would start by loving yourself just as you are. Give yourself a big hug and thank your body for what is still working.

Regarding the pains in the joints, I feel you may need to alter your lifestyle a little. I would start by joining a yoga class to gently stretch your body and improve your flexibility.

I feel that you may have put on a little weight and may need to consider going to Weight Watchers, Slimming World or a similar professional organization that will give you the guidance you need to make the changes in your lifestyle.

Change your diet to mainly fresh fruit and vegetables and take time for your Self to look within and appreciate what is working in your life.

I was once told a lovely story about this very old musician who was about to play a violin solo in a big auditorium, full to capacity with people waiting eagerly to hear this famous musician play.

The old man struggled to get onto the stage and took a few minutes to cross the stage to where he was to sit to pay his violin. He settled himself, and the silence in the room built as he brought the bow up to the instrument and started to play.

Just as he was starting the opening bars there was a load bang as one of the strings on the violin broke. The audience gasped, expecting him to get up and struggle his way back to the dressing room to pick up a spare instrument.

But instead he put the instrument back under his chin and played the most heart-rending piece of music anyone had ever heard.

When he had finished he got a huge standing ovation and, as the clapping gradually subsided, he leaned close to the microphone and said: "In life you have to use what is still working and allow your music to flow through you."

Therefore, I would like to ask you to take this musician's advice and make the most of what you have left in your body that is still working and enjoy your life to the full.

It is never too late to realize your dreams. Take the time to dream and create through your imagination and then allow your energy to flow towards your dream.

While you are dreaming use all your senses to touch, taste, hear and see all the qualities of your dream and aspirations. Then sense what it feels like to have achieved it already, feel the joy and hear the laughter and happiness.

Know that in this process you have already experienced having your desire fulfilled. There is no separation: you have achieved your goal; now see the whole universe working to bring your dream into reality.

54. Chronic Fatigue Syndrome/ME, Insomnia and Other Related Issues—thank you for your question

You are experiencing a change within you that will change the world in which you live. You are a sensitive person; I see this, as you wrote your question about insomnia on the evening of the full moon, when lots of people are wakeful because of the abundance of lunar energy.

What you are going through—although you say a virus causes it—is a subtle change in the world energy patterns.

There is a new awareness coming into being that people are more than their physical bodies; new dimensions and layers of awareness are opening up, which is causing sensitive people like you to feel the pain and fatigue of all human consciousness.

You have chosen to be one of the people to release this for group consciousness. It is a painful and tiring experience, which is leaving you with little energy to do anything else. Know that this is a temporary transition and is nearing its completion.

You can help the process by loving yourself. By this I mean appreciate the work you are doing. This is tougher work than any full time job, and has taken a toll on both your physical and mental health.

The universe does not give you anything you cannot cope with. You are starting to master yourself and love the process which you are going through.

What I would ask you to do is open your Self up more to the process in a loving, friendly way. Improve your "Self-talk" to a more supportive and enabling process to help this change take place within you.

The work you are doing is of immense benefit to mankind and you should love and appreciate all you are doing. You are a very special soul to have been chosen for this work; value yourself with all the love your heart has to give, and give this love back to yourself.

I will send you healing to help you through this process. I would normally ask for a name and location for the healing, but I can feel my heart connected to yours already. Therefore, please accept this love, as I know you are leading the way for many, many more souls to follow into the energy of the New Earth.

You are truly blessed; and so it is.

55. Choosing the Path to Walk by Positive Thinking

The world shows up for us the way we think about it. Choosing clearly what we want in this life is very important. It is important to be clear about our purpose and direction.

Flowing our energy towards a goal and an objective helps, but only if we are coming from the field of love that exists deep in our heart are we in harmony with all life. We need to be true to ourselves first: to be honest about our feelings and intentions and what we want to create in the world.

If our thoughts and desires are positive and life-supporting for ourselves and those around us; if we are coming from the finest layers of our heart's desire, we can honestly know that our thoughts are in tune with the whole universe.

Using the breath to centre our energies and connect with our Higher Self is now easy in the New Energy which has been growing in intensity over the past few years. The coherence and synchrony between people is now becoming so strong that life is flowing without problems as we experience growing support from our environment.

We are truly stepping into the New Earth: a world in which the planet has woken up and become conscious in its own right.

The subtle energies have become like a matrix or web of energy around the planet, creating a field of super-fluid consciousness which interacts with our individual awareness and co-ordinates us all to live in peace and harmony.

As the power of this field grows, we will all awaken out of the sleep-walking we have been doing.

The power of this field will have an effect on us like corn in a hot pan; all of a sudden the corn starts to pop. Human consciousness is the same: conditions are ripe now for us all to start to pop, bursting into a new understanding of who and what we are.

We will move from our localized individual consciousness into a new awareness of our oneness with the whole universe and all the things within it. This is the quantum leap in consciousness, the next rung on the evolutionary ladder to Self-realization.

The nice thing is, it does not require us to go anywhere or do anything: in fact, it is the exact opposite. It is a process of letting go, relaxing and releasing.

Conscious breathing is the secret; by staying conscious of the breath we bring our mind back to the current time zone: the Now, the field where all things are possible and we can choose any thought or dream we may wish to follow.

All fear evaporates in this state; we automatically think positively, as we are coming from the love within our own heart. In this state no-one can tell us what to do, as we know intuitively what the correct action is to take.

We can follow our heart, and now we have the whole universe supporting us every step of the way. You are truly a divine angel looking out from your body.

You will realize that you are immortal and are an expression of the whole; and, even though your body will still follow its natural life cycle, you are aware of your higher nature. Your awareness has moved into the field of energy which is connecting you to the whole planet and expanding outwards to the whole universe.

Your awareness has transcended your physical existence: you have dropped down the layers of the body; down through the organs, the cells, the molecules, the atoms into the quantum particles and beyond matter itself: into the neutral energy of pure awareness.

Aware of the field of empty time and Space which underlies our physical universe, you become a free spirit not localized in your body any more but able to travel the universe at will. The beauty is, though, that you do not have to travel anywhere, as you are there already: you just choose to move your awareness around.

Your awareness merges with life itself, the source of all creation: you have aligned your energy with nature and become God. You are a divine human; your thoughts are the thoughts of the whole universe, the oneness of the Self in harmony with the divine creator.

Enjoy your new awareness: watch all your friends pop like popcorn and come and join you on the New Earth; welcome home.

56. Drawing on the Energies at Ancient Sites

It's as though a sixth sense wakes up as you come close to an ancient monument or special area of nature; you can feel the presence in the energies. At one of these areas on our planet, if you take a few minutes to pause in the daily rush to achieve, and just be still, you can feel the deeper connection and get a sense of the history of the site.

If it's a dry day and you can sit on the ground and make a connection to the Earth, you can feel the energy of the area flowing around and through you. You may feel this in many ways: you may get a sense of the sounds made there in the distant past, and feel the wind on your face in a special way.

What I notice myself, as I sit and start to drift into a meditative state, is that the energies in my face become more pronounced. I get a kind of silly little grin forming and I feel the field of energy within my body and out into the aura becoming stronger and more charged up.

I become like a radio tuner with its base frequency which can amplify small fluctuations in the surrounding energies. As you tune into nature and imagine roots going down into the ground to earth your energy field, you become sensitive to the slightest change in your environment.

As you reach out with your feeling and sense the energies, you can choose what aspect of the energies you would like to tune into. You may want to allow your awareness to drift back a thousand years and feel what was happening in this area then.

As you sit there with your eyes closed you may find your sixth sense becoming active; you may start to see images in your imagination or hear sounds, smell the smoke of a campfire or taste the food that was cooking.

You may become aware of the quality of the energy and its mood. Is it happy energy or is there some other quality?

You may want to project your awareness forward and see how the interesting features and natural beauty of the area could be enhanced. You can use your imagination to create the blueprint for the nature spirits to work with to bring your dream into reality.

As you tune in deeper to the energies and allow your boundaries to become fuzzy; as you become one with nature, you attune to the vibration of the area and the interplay of the five elements of Fire, Earth, Air, Water and the Life Force itself.

You may sense the presence of the nature spirits or elves, angels, spirit guides...

Using your imagination and feeling you could start up a conversation with them and discuss any areas of interest.

You may notice that you are also getting very deep relaxation and inspiration at the same time. To join to nature you have to tune your energies in and become one with nature. This has a very balancing and healing effect on you.

Some parts of the world are renowned for the healing properties of their energies. Know that it is the energies in your body that do the adjusting and balancing. Know also that this is a process of letting go, relaxing and releasing.

It is a process of moving out of your head and your intellect into your heart and your feeling and just being one with your body, nature and your Higher Self.

The nice thing is, as we allow our attention to go to these subtle layers of nature, we allow nature to merge with our awareness. As it does so, nature itself can become aware of its own essence and the whole planet can start to wake up and know itself.

This is the process of planetary Ascension: a re-merging of all the different aspects of ourselves. Parts that we have felt were separate start to become aware of their unified nature and the oneness of life itself.

57. Feel Your Inner Body

We all know we have a physical body, but today I would like you to start to become aware of your Inner Body or Energy Body.

The Inner Body we could say is the energy field which permeates and surrounds our physical body.

This Inner Body contains the blueprint which the physical body grows into.

When our awareness is on the physical level of our body we are mainly concerned with its physical attributes, but true beauty comes from within. When our subtle energies are strong we radiate this love all around us.

Strong subtle energies create more orderliness in the physical body, leading to better health and a more contented nature. People may comment that we have strong charisma as they feel this energy radiating from us.

So how do we make this inner Energy Body stronger? Well, there are many spiritual practices that claim to do this. You may do it through yoga and meditation or a myriad of other techniques.

What I feel works best is just to become conscious of it, as what we put our attention on, grows.

You can feel this energy easily by just bringing the palms of your hands together slowly. When they get to between 6 and 3 inches apart you start to feel subtle sensations in your hands. This is a way to feel the subtle energy like a magnetic field surrounding our body.

This aura of energy which we live in, that forms part of our con-sciousness and feelings, permeates through our physical body as well.

If we allow our awareness to go within we can feel our body from the inside. A simple way to do this is to scan through the body with the aware-ness, releasing any tension in the muscles and joints as we go.

Whenever we feel any tension in the body it is a good idea to take the consciousness within and consciously release that tension and relax the muscles.

This process of relaxing and releasing tension allows the body to settle down and grow in wholeness.

This wholeness or oneness of the body is very healing and allows the whole body to feel at peace with itself.

If you expand your feelings outwards and connect with the Earth energies and the planets of our solar system just through your intention and imagination, you can feel at peace with the world and the whole universe around you.

Breathing is another way to reach this state of inner peace and relaxation.

By becoming conscious of the breath as it enters and leaves our nose we start to become aware of the Prana or Life Force coming in with each breath. If, through your intention, you breathe this Life Force into each part of your body, you can easily become aware of this inner field of energy.

This is also a good way to detach from the ego-nature of the mind as, from this level of inner being, we start to witness the dramas that are playing out in our lives and we see that we are independent of the drama and free to choose how we want to be, think and feel.

We start to realize we have a choice as to how we react to situations. This realization gives us immense freedom to be and act in whatever way we choose, as we are feeling at peace and relaxed.

In this state we tend to react to events in a more peaceful and knowing way, whereby we can make decisions with a clearer mind and more awareness of what we would like to create in that moment.

We become naturally a more loving, caring person with a clearer mind and a healthier body. Our personal energy is much stronger and we are less influenced by others.

It is as though we develop an inner frame of reference which allows the synchronies of the universe to come about. We just find ourselves in the right place at the right time for something magical to happen and for our life to take on a new evolutionary direction without effort.

58. Inner Work and Stepping into the New Consciousness

Reflect a moment on the changes that have taken place in your life over the past few months. How many of your favourite things have you had to release and let go of?

Have you noticed the change in your inner awareness? Have you noticed a greater depth to your feelings and awareness?

As we move into the New Energy of Oneness and expand our awareness and consciousness, we see lots of past issues coming to the surface, again, to be finally released, and our energies are more centred on our inner awareness and inner development.

You may find that your awareness rests on past issues, and you have strong thoughts associated with those events. Take a deep breath and clear. [The term "clear" just has the effect of releasing the energies you have been holding onto. I just feel a release as I use this technique.]

Stay conscious of your breathing for a minute or two, and look again at that thought. See the illusion within it: it is not of this time frame, therefore thank it and then release it and focus your energies in the Now; be with yourself and become aware of your feelings.

Scan your feelings for any tension and release that as well. You may notice a new inner quiet developing; let your awareness be with this for a few seconds and explore its qualities. You may feel an inner joy, a feeling of bliss as you put your attention on the Silence within.

Whenever you find yourself thinking thoughts which are not relevant to the moment of Now, take a deep breath and clear. If you find you are thinking thoughts that you are not enjoying and did not consciously create: Think again. Use the field of all possibilities within to create your most perfect thought for this moment.

You have the power to think any thought you desire, so choose the thoughts which bring you upliftment, and release and clear. Through conscious breathing release any thoughts which can be classed as negative.

Focus on what you want. A lot of people put their attention on what is not working and expand that experience in their life. What you put your attention on grows and expands; therefore choose clearly what is your heart's dream and what your desires are, and consciously breathe your energies into that experience.

Rebalance your energies and allow them to flow freely towards your dreams and aspirations. See the fear drop away as you do this and centre your energies on your heart centre, your feelings, and come from love.

You can now feel the presence of a new reality developing on the Earth, a new world which you are helping to create. Feel your connection to the Earth beneath your feet; stay connected and grounded over the coming year. Welcome the changes that are happening.

Embrace your feelings and follow your heart's desire; step forward into the new world.

59. Know Yourself as Eternal, Non-Changing and Absolute

As you are walking along the seashore listening to the eternal sound of the waves breaking on the beach, your mind could be a million miles away, being aware of the eternal continuum of life, but in reality just knowing your true nature.

As we walk through life we see the constant change around us as everything follows its natural life cycle.

Our body is no exception: it is constantly changing—growing and evolving. Yet the person within the body, that silent witness to all we experience, has an eternal quality of something much greater and more permanent than who or what we think we are.

In our quiet moments when we are walking or sitting with nature, our feelings reach out and connect and touch a deeper layer of our heart and soul. We become in union with that hidden force that orders the whole of creation.

We can be one with this field of love, this presence of the divine which is within us and surrounding us in each moment of our lives. All we need to do is just be present, and our awareness will naturally settle and become one with its divine nature.

We leave behind our physical nature and connect with that presence of love that underlies the physical. We connect with our true Self, the silent witness to our life and experiences.

That which was never born can never die. Our true Self is the eternal continuum of Life itself. What happens in our life is here just for a few moments; we are connected to the whole of life. We can choose any experience we wish to have in each moment, just by choosing that experience with the next breath we take.

You have come to Earth for a divine purpose, to have an experience and to create your dreams with your imagination. Next time you are out in nature take the time to reflect on what your dream is; what you have chosen to create in this lifetime.

Ask yourself what your true nature is. Like any plant in the garden, we are all unique. We have come into this world with a specific DNA: a blueprint for life. A rosebud can only grow into a rose, and so with a daisy bud. What is your nature?

We surround ourselves with a loving, nurturing atmosphere. We are here to grow and develop just like the plants in the garden. We have been allocated a life cycle, just like the plants. This is not a dress rehearsal: it is life itself.

What is your dream? What is your passion? What difference do you want to create and express in this lifetime? We are all different: we all have a different nature and a different dream to live.

We are not here to copy anyone; we are here to express our nature, live our dream and be the finest example of who and what we wish to create in this lifetime.

So, next time you are feeling connected to your soul and at peace with the whole universe, allow your Higher Self to guide you on your path to your true destiny. Dream your dream, and live your life expressing your Joy and blossoming into your full nature.

60. Loneliness: What is the Cause, and How do we Overcome it in Our Lives?

Many people experience loneliness in their lives, at some stage. As children we mix and make friends easily but as we get older and more fixed in our ways, we may find it more challenging to find like-minded people we feel comfortable with.

To overcome loneliness is one of modern society's issues today. With television tending to portray fear and stress in their drama productions, one can get conditioned into becoming introverted, especially if one lives alone.

There are a few things we can do to help reverse this tendency in later life, and that is to consider all the things we enjoy doing. Then ask at the Library, or find a What's-On-type publication, to see what clubs and societies there are nearby which engage in these interests.

If your interest is not catered for, consider being the source of that interest by starting your own club or society to pursue it. It is also a good idea to have a go at new things.

A year back I decided I was going to join a new club or society each month and see how I got on. I am glad I did this as I got lots of experience of new things, met lots of new people and gained a greater awareness of life and living.

These days I am never at home: I am always out visiting different groups and societies. This has really improved my confidence and self-esteem and I am sure it can do the same for you.

Taking an active role in the community can also help. Consider sharing your expertise with the young, either by offering to teach at home or going to youth clubs. We have all got something to give: it is just a question of taking a few minutes to reflect on what these areas are.

When you have assessed what you are good at and what you have to offer, look for areas where people come together. A lot of communities have an officer in charge of organising community events: go and have a word with them and see what can be worked out.

Shyness is a bit like selfishness: we hold ourselves back and block ourselves from giving. Put your attention on what you can do and think much less about what you can't do and the things that block you. Then watch your energies flow feely and real progress start to be made in your desires and aspirations.

If you are housebound think of putting a notice in the local shop for a visitor to came and chat for an hour or two per day.

When doing this think positively, as we attract to us the way we feel. If we raise our feeling frequency so we are happy and at peace with the world then we will attract to us like-minded people that will be uplifting to be with.

The best way then to stop feeling lonely is to start to approach life with enthusiasm and go out and start connecting in whatever way you feel inspired.

❧

61. How does one know the difference between needing to be patient for Spirit to manifest something and needing to change something in what one is doing? I get confused about needing to let go and allow success and prosperity come on their own terms, versus having to do more to actively catalyse a result that I desire.

Spirit cannot act on its own and it will not do our work for us. Therefore it is important to know what you want for yourself.

The first stage of creation is to dream or visualize with the subtle thinking processes of the mind. Then start to move towards that which you desire; and, if you are in tune with the Universal Life Force, your desire will soon gain fulfilment.

The other word you use is "need". The body needs certain things to survive and live a comfortable life, but I think what you are referring to here is "desire". You desire to manifest something in your life, whether it is a new partner, or a job you enjoy, or a change in your home, or a holiday, or whatever else it is you desire.

The point is, it is not a basic need: it is something you would like to have because the thought about it brings you pleasure.

What is important is your state of mind: if you feel a separation from your need or desire, that is what you will experience. The world shows up the way we think about it.

The key is to think in such a way that you already have that which you desire within you, so that there is no separation. This really is a question of who or what you think you are.

If you feel that you are your physical body and everything outside of yourself is separate and different from you, then you will feel this lack and separation.

But, if you look at yourself in a higher way and feel that you are a part of the Universal Life Force and that everything you see around you is just a different aspect of yourself, without any separation, just a continuous stream of energy flowing freely; you may start to see the subtle difference I am making.

The thing about life is, if you wait for Spirit to manifest something for you, the whole universe waits with you. If you take the first step towards that which you desire, the whole universe moves to fulfil your desire. It is just a question of your intention, and who and what you think you are.

The other part of your question seems to be about abundance in your life. Quite often abundance and joy go together. Therefore I would say that if you are not enjoying what you are doing then abundance might not show up for you.

But if you choose what really makes your heart sing, what you have a strong desire to do; then, if you follow your passion and bring into the physical world what you desire, this may also, after a while, bring abundance into your life, too.

The secret is to do what you enjoy and have a passion for, and move towards it, and watch the whole universe move to fulfil that joyous thought.

62. Our Destiny is in the Planets and Stars

As we grow in awareness of who and what we are, we start to become aware of the influence of the planets and stars on the flow of our life. For thousands of years people have been aware of the subtle effect of the planets in our solar system and their influence on our moods and destiny.

Astrologers have followed the movement of the planets and their relationship to events in our life. This knowledge has led to the creating of astrology, a system to predict future events in our life from the position of the planets at our birth.

If you look into the Kabala system of knowledge—an ancient Jewish mystical tradition—you will see that each heavenly body is given the name of an archangel and we can call upon their influence to bring changes in our life.

Each planet is known for its qualities: Venus—the planet of Love, Mars—the planet of War, and so on. These influences set a direction which is the natural flow of life. But it is not fixed, and in every moment of our life, we can use our free will to create our own future and destiny.

What I am bringing out is the multi-dimensional nature of being human. There are many forces interacting with our body each and every day. The energy field of our body is like a cosmic computer interpreting these influences and always aiming to reach a balance.

We can always use our free will to shape these influences and, using our imagination, create a different dream or path to follow.

You are always given a choice to go with the flow of life or create something different, something new, and flow your energies in a different way. Neither is right or wrong, they are just different paths to walk.

Lots of people use gemstones or crystals to enhance the influence of a certain planet. The chakras, the energy vortices of the body, work like radio tuners picking up the energy that is being radiated by the planets, each tuning in to its distinct frequency.

It is good now and again to just relax and let the mind and the body come to peace within themselves, either through meditation or something as simple as fishing or knitting.

As we let go of our ego controlling everything, our energies naturally find their own balance and we become more alert to these subtle influences which are permeating our environment.

As we tune in to the cosmic dance and align our energies with that, we become more in tune with these subtle influences, so they start to support and co-ordinate our life. We find that they are also giving the same massages to our neighbours and we notice that synchronies start to happen.

We receive the support of the whole universe in every thought, word and deed that flows from us.

These synchronies are co-ordinated and we find that problems naturally drop away from us, as we let go of controlling through our ego. We start to be aware of the subtle energies and feelings that inspire us to action in a natural way.

Self-awareness and becoming conscious of all these subtle influences are bringing a new, deeper connection to the oneness of the energies of which we are a part. As we tune in, so we feel the peace and harmony, and life flows in a happier, more joyful way.

This is all about moving the awareness from the intellect, in the head, down to your feelings, in your heart; living your life from the love radiating from your heart in full awareness.

63. Stopping Smoking and Balancing Your Weight

The thing about stopping smoking (as people typically do it) is, they put their attention on the stopping, which the human mind tends to interpret as a block. As the mind wants to feel free and unbounded, this is against its nature. In answer to a question

Therefore if you truly desire to stop, you will do this naturally :>)

What I would suggest is that you decide what you would like to do instead of smoking? What new desires you would like to explore and dream about, to pay for with the money that you save from naturally wanting to improve your health?

You will also substitute an activity that is destructive to your body for a constructive one, by moving away from poisoning your body through the inhalation of poisonous gases.

This is a very personal thing and only you know what brings you greatest happiness and joy. My own advice if I were to offer some would be to look within your Self, find your own inner dream which you have always wanted to do, and go and do it.

Regarding avoiding weight gain: if you create a vision of your perfect weight in your mind's eye and set this up as a blueprint for your body to grow into, you will naturally have a balanced weight.

Some tips that may help:

Eat only when you are hungry.

Drink lots of water.

Have your main meal at lunchtime and only eat a small snack in the evening.

Eat food with the Life Force in it: i.e. mainly fresh fruit and vegetables.

I wish you luck on choosing a new way forward for your life. I am happy that you will follow your dream and experience the freedom of choosing what you want in your life consciously.

You have made a big choice already in wanting to improve the way you live your life, by naturally allowing the negative tendencies to drop away, putting your attention fully on what you do want and allowing your energies to flow freely towards that goal.

ॐ

64. Strands of Consciousness are Growing in our Awareness

When you use your imagination to create a dream, or germinate a new concept or idea, your consciousness becomes multi-dimensional. You may think that you are just thinking subtle thoughts in your mind, but each thought is connected to a different dimension in an alternate reality.

Self awareness of our consciousness is developing its multi-dimensional nature.

To date you may have considered your mind as flat and thoughts just appear out of nowhere. Now the field of consciousness is getting so strong that, if you relax and expand you awareness through your feeling, you will become aware of the multi-dimensional nature of your awareness and thinking process.

You will start to feel the connection to distant realities, where you have different aspects of yourself. Here you plan and dream in the subtle levels of consciousness.

You will become aware of the tapestry of consciousness; where, instead of being flat, there is an infinite web of threads of consciousness connecting all aspects together in a flowing matrix of light.

Perhaps the closest example of this concept is the Internet, where data is stored in separate locations on servers around the world. Yet each of these locations is connected by a web of fibre optic cables or copper wires, which allow a search engine to call up any data you may choose to ask for.

In this same way, knowledge is stored in the Akashic records and in distant galaxies in an infinite web of thoughts and feelings, which the brain translates into impulses of light that go into and come out of the underlying field of neutral energy. This field, which is like an empty vacuum or void, links the whole omniverse together.

This field is omnipresent and underlies physical creation; it is super fluid and contains infinite possibilities.

When light enters this field it changes form and speeds up many thousands of times to a soup or web so fine and complex that any data can be processed, even before the thought has had time to grow and take form in the mind.

This is the subtlest level of the thinking process we have become conscious of to date. It is the Internet of the omniverse, a matrix that transcends all physical matter in the human, plant and animal kingdoms.

To connect to this field you do not have to do anything, as it is your true nature. It is a process of letting go and relaxing and falling back on the Self. Just to read this is enough to bring it to your awareness; and your awareness will make the connection to this field in its own way and its own time.

Group consciousness has now risen to a level where this awareness is becoming commonplace. Enjoy exploring the finer levels of your awareness through your feelings.

65. Tantric Healing Enriches Relationships

Healing can be on many levels, and one of the main areas for healing is human relationships. Tantric Healing is the balancing and feeling of the Divine Life Force as we draw it through us and radiate it to our partner.

Tantra is the flow of energy from our most subtle core, through all our five senses, balancing the Yin-Yang (Male-Female) energy, as we weave our cosmic dance on the stage of life.

Tantra can be practised with each of the senses and in everything we do; it is a process of being aware and fully present to each moment of experience.

You can practise Tantra while enjoying a meal in a fine restaurant, just being aware of all the subtle sensations of your taste buds and experiencing the look, colours, texture and aroma of the food and wine.

You can practise Tantra while listening to music or visiting the art gallery or museum; it is all about connecting to your subtle feelings and gaining more depth from the experience by being aware and present on many levels at the same time.

People over the years have trained to develop their awareness through yoga and meditation. They have:

- become aware of the subtle energy centres in the body—the Chakras;
- trained to experience the rising of the Kundalini and the flow of the Life Force;
- and learned sets of postures and rituals to blend the Yin-Yang strands of the Life Force together and generate a whole symphony of experiences leading to self-realization from the union of sharing.

Tantra is about openness and looking into unexplored areas of life in a non-judgemental way. It is about transcending belief systems; freeing the spirit from past experience; and shining consciousness in full awareness in the present moment.

During the practice of Tantra you can look in great depth at what you are feeling and experiencing while giving in a sharing way the Divine Life Force which you are.

The auras merge and the electromagnetic field of the body grows in strength, creating a charisma, a field of love, which surrounds, permeates and envelops the two partners in healing warmth.

If you feel your relationship with your partner could be improved, think of positive ways you could discuss this with your partner and get their help in enriching the physical experience of sharing your love with each other.

Tantra is all about using the full range of your senses from the everyday surface level to the subtle depth of your core being.

Partners can swap roles and the female can play a dominating role, enhancing the masculine side of her nature, while the male is passive and experiences the flow of more feminine energy. This helps to bring balance to the Yin-Yang and healing.

The range of experiences is limited only by our imagination and the extent to which we are awake, present and connected to our senses in the moment.

It is all about giving to each other to create a cosmic dance of experience to savour and share. The giving creates abundance of feelings and vibrations which the senses absorb and grow in richness and love.

As the experience deepens, the Yin-Yang come into balance and something greater than the sum of the parts is created: an awareness of oneness and union with the Divine.

⁂

66. The Connection Point Between the Physical and the Non-Physical Consciousness

As you get ready to settle down to go to sleep at night, you may start to be aware of the connection between your physical body and your non-physical spiritual nature or aura surrounding and permeating through your body.

The junction point between different states of consciousness—i.e. waking and sleeping—is a good time to notice this experience.

As your mind and body start to settle down to rest, you become aware of the more subtle nature of the body, mind and aura. For me this experience is one of first scanning my body and my feelings and becoming aware of my deeper connection.

If I become aware of any discomfort in the body, I take my attention into that region and consciously breathe, relaxing the physical body and clearing the mind of any associated thoughts.

As you continue with this process, you may become aware of a third level of awareness: a field of energy similar to magnetism, which both surrounds and permeates the mind and the body.

This field of energy is the aura, the energy field of the body. It has consciousness too and you may notice your awareness passing from the physical body to the non-physical aura as you settle down to sleep.

Sometimes I experience this as clouds of white light washing over the body and passing through it.

As you take your awareness from your physical body and step over and become aware of your feelings as being within the clouds of white mist of the aura, you notice a freeing of your awareness: an expansion and slight rising of your frequency.

The human body is such a wonderful thing, as we can experience it on many levels and see the connections into many different aspects or dimensions of its nature.

As we become aware of this non-physical connection to our Higher Self we may also become aware of its nature.

We could invite in our guides and angels to come around us. We could take a few minutes just appreciating the work they do for us. We could start to ask them for guidance or plan what we would like to do or experience tomorrow.

This is a magical time as we start to drift off into sleep and, if you witness your sleep, you may even have the experience of your spiritual awareness going out of body and astral travelling through the universe.

This is all a part of your Higher Self: the clouds of white light that you feel are your spiritual connection into the non-physical world.

This non-physical nature, although it is not localized like your body, is still as much a part of who you are as the physical nature of your body: in fact I would say it is more your true nature.

So next time you are going to sleep, just in an innocent way remain aware of your feelings and experiences and consciously enjoy being aware of the many aspects of who and what you are.

67. Transmute Anger and Fear into a Positive New Direction with Passion and Desire

Anger and Fear have been around a very long time as emotions, driving us in directions we may not want to go in and often regret. By becoming aware of these deep emotions we can ask ourselves: are they still serving us? Using passion for life and our desire, we can create a new future direction for our life.

Quite often, if we look deeply at what is making us angry, it can be difficult to identify why we are reacting in this way. It is almost as though we were doing it out of habit or re-enacting a previous situation. Or it could be as simple as: we have always reacted in this way. But why?

By becoming aware of our feeling and questioning what we are doing and why, we bring this subconscious reaction to our conscious mind. We can choose from a field of all possible actions in that moment, what we want to create.

Again, fear is also an interesting emotion which does not stand up to being questioned. What we fear tends to be a projection either into the past or the future: it very rarely appears in the current time frame.

Fear, again, needs to be examined as it can block our actions and cause us to hold back or to act in an avoiding way, which may not fully serve what we want to achieve. Fear is sometimes referred to as "False Evidence Appearing Real": when you look steadily at it, the evidence dissolves away before your very eyes.

Therefore there is an urgent need to look at these two emotions and see if they are holding us back in life.

Passion for what we enjoy, and our Soul Purpose, are what drive us in life and create our desires to achieve. More and more people are choosing their job not for the money but because it fulfils their passion and Soul Purpose.

Also, real abundance tends to come in our life when we give freely of our passion. One tends to find that those who enjoy their work give freely and are very creative because they enjoy what they are doing.

Therefore, take a few minutes each day to question your angers and fears. Look at what you are passionate about regarding these issues and see if there is a more constructive way of reaching the goal.

Use your dreams and imagination to create new possibilities for your Self. Then step your life into those dreams and realize a new life's purpose for yourself. Live your life in a more fulfilling, purposeful way which brings joy to your Self and those around you.

68. Death and How it Affects the Living

When we talk about life and death it is necessary for us to question who and what we are? What life is all about and how we interact with each other?

Life is something very subtle within the body. It is the Life Force that holds all the different parts of the body together and gives purpose and direction to life. Yet the experience of life is one of being the observer to what is happening in our environment and body.

We know that we are not the physical body because every cell in the body changes every 7 years, yet the personality within the body stays the same from a small baby to a teenager to an adult.

We are spiritual in nature; you could say the Self is an angel who looks out from the body and sees and senses the world around us through this vehicle we call our body. I would even go as far as to say that I believe the angel within the Soul of the person was never born and therefore can never die.

From physics' point of view I would say the Self is unmanifest, like the vacuum state in quantum physics, which is an eternal continuum—never changing, always the same.

This unmanifest state is connected to the whole universe but at the same time takes on a local quality, which forms the soul of the person. By "soul" I don't mean anything separate from the person; it is just a way of talking about them that denotes that they are eternal.

I like to use the analogy of the air in the room. Each room has a different smell to it and different qualities in the air, yet there is no point where the air in one room ends and the air of the next room begins: they are joined, yet different.

What I am basically saying is that the soul of the person was never born, i.e. never became manifest in physical form, and therefore can never die. It always was a part of the eternal continuum of life that underlies this physical world and the body which it was looking through while we referred to the body in normal terms as alive.

So, if you have managed to follow my thought this far, you can see that the soul of the person is a part of the eternal continuum and, after shedding this body, may choose to step into the next body and start a new life over again.

As regards the living relatives left behind after a loved one has shed the body, I feel it is up to each one of us to see and react to this event however we choose. There is no right or wrong way to react to the death of a loved one.

All I would like to say on the subject is that the deceased are only a thought away. You may have had the experience of telepathy with a close loved one while they were alive. You may even have had the feeling of their loss before you were told at what time the death did occur.

All I am saying is that we are connected to the ones we love on a soul level and we can communicate with them on a soul level.

I would also like to say, it is not what happens in our life or what happens to our loved ones that makes the difference. It is how we react to what happens in our life that makes all the difference in the world. Each one of us is in control of our reaction: we have the choice to think any thought in any moment.

Therefore, you may wish to question how you are reacting to the death of a close loved one and see if it is serving you? Is it making any difference to the person who has died? Or would a loving thought felt deep in the heart and sent out to that person have a more constructive effect?

If you allow yourself to connect to the person who has died and send them loving thoughts, you may find that you get a feeling back of that person coming around you. You may feel them as an angel around you helping to comfort you in this time of mourning.

Therefore, please let go of all the mystery of death, as there is no such thing, only the taking on of a body and then shedding it. This does not affect the dweller within the body one bit, as they stay in the eternal continuum of life all the time.

If your beliefs around this subject cause you suffering, please look into them: in some religions, such as spiritualism, the survival of life after death causes much rejoicing.

Lots of souls are choosing to leave the body at this time. Their work on Earth is finished for now; but life goes on, and they will be back in a new role and a new dimension to discover more about life and living and the evolutionary process of ascension.

69. Memories and Emotions can Colour our Awareness

Memories have an emotional charge that can colour our awareness. These emotions can make us react in strange ways following certain triggers. You may find yourself becoming aware of a past event's memory and notice that you are looking back and not fully present with what is going on around you now.

Memories of past events in our life can hold a strong emotional charge.

This can cause these memories to keep repeating themselves over and over again throughout our life.

Sometimes the pattern is triggered by our environment and at other times by a person or situation. Once triggered, the memory of the event plays out, with all the pent-up emotional charge of the original event.

The first step to solving this pattern of behaviour is to become aware of the process. If you find your mood swinging for no apparent reason it may be that one of these past memories is playing out at a subconscious level.

By focusing on what is happening, you are bringing it back into the conscious mind and questioning the validity of the emotions you are experiencing.

Through forgiveness we can release the energies that are stuck in this pattern of experience and behaviour. Through forgiveness we release the emotional charge, whether it has to do with yourself, another person, or an event.

These memory patterns can keep playing out over long periods of time and create shadows which stop us seeing the true reality of a situation. As we move into the New Energy more of these patterns of behaviour are coming up to the surface of the mind to be released.

As we release each one, we become a little more aware of the true reality around us. We become a little more centred within ourselves and aware of what is happening now, and receive genuine information from our senses.

This growth in our awareness and expansion of our feelings and emotions allows us to grow in self-knowledge. It gives us the freedom to choose our mood first and come from our own heart centre and radiate love to those around us.

We stop reacting to life, and start to create the life we would love to experience and grow into.

We empower ourselves to see life as it truly is and enjoy it in the moment, without carrying all the baggage of past events with us. We become a master of ourselves and therefore master the way we see and experience the world in which we live.

We are growing in mastery and enjoying living life in an evolutionary way. This growth is happening now on an individual level. Soon we will see it happening in our communities and on the level of government, and it will grow into a new awareness in the world of the oneness of life.

70. "My Biggest Problem is that I Feel Deeply Connected to Suffering"

You live in a field of opposites. All around you are—up and down, hot and cold, good and bad, joy and suffering. One defines the other; we cannot know anything without the contrast or the opposite being present.

The question is: what do you want to put your attention on and thus make grow?

Life would be very boring if everything were the same. That is why we have created the contrast in life. What I am asking you to do is see the unity in the contrast and decide where you want to put your attention.

Is your glass half full or half empty? If you put your attention on the half empty you will spiral down until you know the depths of emptiness. If you put your attention on a half full glass you will spiral up until your glass is overflowing with life and love.

"I have scarce resources myself so I can't help by sharing in a financial way"—I get the feeling that you are dis-empowering yourself.

You could choose to be the source of abundance for another person. Even with the little you have it is very easy for you to find someone who has even less than you and share your abundance with him or her.

Do you see the change in mindset? You are the universe, so you have no lack unless you forget to remember who you are!

"The beauty and yet the pain of the Now"—When we go to a cinema to watch a film, it may be about happiness, it may be about sadness. It could be the most violent war film or the most touching love story, but in all cases the film screen is just the silent witness.

It does not get caught up in the film: it is just the screen on which it is shown. It is the same with your mind. Your mind is the screen on which the film of life is shown in all its contrasts.

The personality within the body—the Self—is non-changing, absolute, and is just the silent witness to life.

You have the freedom to choose your reaction to life in every moment. You can choose to take on the pain and suffering; or you can choose to be the silent witness and react in a positive way to create the change you wish to experience.

71. Protection while Healing: A Step-by-Step Guide

How can I be certain that I am fully protecting myself when giving healing?

This question came up at our Healers' Circle during a training session recently.

The general consensus in our healing group was, as long as you ask to be connected to the highest, purest energy to give healing, and ground yourself afterwards, no harm should come to you.

The healers thought it beneficial to say an opening prayer asking for protection and to be connected to the highest energy, asking for our healing helpers and guides to come and join us in the healing.

Some thought it also useful to open the energy centres in the body (the chakras) to aid the flow of energy.

After the healing session the healers were suggesting to wash through their auras with white light and ground their energy field. Some of the healers were saying they could feel in themselves during healing the imbalances of the person they were giving healing to—this is where the grounding comes in.

Some suggested doing this by standing barefoot on wet grass, or in a running stream, or taking a shower and visualising the stale energy leaving the system in the water as it passed over them.

Others in the group thought that just visualising grounding roots growing from your feet was enough to ground the energy field.

The general feeling was that each person has his or her preferred system for doing this and that it was good practice to get in the routine of clearing the healer's aura after each session.

If your true Self is all that is contained in the universe, then what is there to fear, except fear itself?

72. How Does Our Consciousness Change as we Evolve and Become More Spiritual?

An understanding of how we can break the cycle of cause and effect and gain stability in our lives

The main change we notice is from being caught up in an individual thought, and having it take over our entire mind, to having a more expanded view on life. When we get a very strong thought—especially a negative one—it can sweep us along and later we can find that we have done things that we really did not want to do.

To avoid this happening it is possible to experience thoughts on different levels. I.e. if a strong unpleasant thought comes into the mind, take the mind to the physical body and you may experience a twitching or sensation in one or more parts of the body.

Just let the mind experience that sensation for a little while. Think of that area of the body regaining balance and harmony. When the sensation eases take the mind back to the thinking process and you will find that those strong emotions have passed.

Through this process you have managed to break the cycle of action and reaction that continues to cause these tensions to build up in our bodies.

It is also noticeable that as the mind expands, this is when the consciousness starts to experience more at the same time. Therefore each individual thought occupies a much smaller part of our consciousness.

If you can imagine the mind as like the ocean and our consciousness and thoughts like the waves of the ocean then, as our mind becomes conscious of the more subtle layers, we get more depth to it.

You start to take in more of the silent layers of the ocean so that you have the waves and you have the still water under the waves at the same time.

73. Marketing in Business and Commerce in the New Consciousness

As we move into the New Consciousness, business will change from selfish accumulation to giving and sharing, thus creating abundance for everyone and balance in the world economy. In answer to a question.

I sense that you are still feeling a little separated from your customers. You are shifting your focus from your own income, to giving to customers, to help their lives grow and blossom. I think you are still missing the point.

The point is, what you give to another, you give to yourself: the reason being that there is only one of us. You are a part of the Universal Life Force just the same as your customer is. If you want to have any experience in your life, just cause another to have that experience, and you notice it showing up in your life as well.

We have had the Industrial Revolution; now we are going through a consciousness revolution. The boundary between where your consciousness ends and your customer's begins is falling away. People are becoming more intuitive and telepathic.

The consciousness of the planet is waking up and each individual mind is starting to realize that it is part of a bigger system. As the energy of the Oneness grows, so does synchrony in your life, where you find your Self in the right place at the right time for something magical to happen.

The path of life is marked out by your Joy, and all of us have a field of all possibilities open to us in each moment: at every step on the path to evolution and growth, just choose what brings you greatest joy from all these possible options.

You need to ask the question, "Can wealth create on its own, or do we create the wealth?" It is human consciousness that expresses the Divine Life Force which flows through us and gives birth to our desires and passions; that comes into reality in our thoughts, words and actions.

Open up and connect your own individual life's purpose to the purpose of the divine Universal Life Force that causes growth in each individual and in the whole system of business and commerce.

Very soon the business system is going to realize that it is no longer about profit. It is about growth, sharing and helping bring balance to the whole planet.

There is no longer a need for Microsoft to have 57 billion dollars in the bank, while millions starve in Africa. This is like saying it is great that my brain has all this money, while my leg withers and dies through starvation.

Balance, and helping the whole to develop and grow together, is our future path. We just have to release the fear of shortage in world resources, and transform it into giving and sharing what we are all a part of: Life itself. We just need to wake up to the bigger picture.

&

74. Releasing Fear and Growing in Joy and Happiness

As we move more into the New Energy and expand our awareness of life and living, we are growing in love and releasing fear.

Just allow yourself to smile; you do not need a reason. As you smile, sense the depth of that smile with your feeling. Start with the smile on your face and feel the warmth of its energy expanding to take in the whole of your body. Consciously take a few deep breaths.

Feel the depth of the smile as you become aware of all the organs in the body smiling; feel the cells within the organs start to smile and express their love. Feel all the molecules within the cells start to smile, and feel the atoms that make up the molecules beam a really big deep smile.

Feel your energy balancing with the warmth of this love. Just connect to that feeling of love that underlies our atoms; feel the neutral energy, which is hidden from science because it has no qualities.

Become aware of the vacuum or void that underlies this physical universe: that eternal continuum which is never-changing, yet is the source of all change. Just be in awareness of who you are.

You are the Life Force of Creation: you are the Non-Changing which flows out into this field of constant change. As you open up to this love deep within your heart, allow your awareness to connect to it. Feel your frequency rise as you start to merge your awareness with Life itself.

Allow this love to flow through you from the finest layer of your being out through your body, bringing all your body's layers of energy into perfect balance and harmony.

Visualize all the finer particles merging and forming the atoms; the atoms merging and forming the molecules; the molecules merging and forming the cells; the cells merging and forming the organs, nerves and bones. See all the layers and all the parts forming in the whole of you.

Feel your whole body being at peace with the world, your awareness fully alert and awake to who you are. As your energies come into balance, see all your life flow freely without resistance. What you need is already flowing to you even before you have thought of it.

You are part of a much larger system. See and feel your energy grow in awareness. Know that you are living a synchronous life, where what you need shows up in your Space at exactly the right moment.

Have faith in the system of which you are a part. Allow your energy to expand and flow freely. Use your imagination, dreams and aspirations to guide you to your field of Joy. Wake up to who you are.

You are Life itself, ever-flowing, eternal; there is no separation between you and God. You are God, creating and flowing. Feel your love and your connection to the whole universe, and live in peace and harmony with the other aspects of yourself.

75. Your Relationship with Yourself is Equally Important

We sometimes identify with the things that happen in our life but, really, we are always free to love ourselves.

Before we can have a meaningful relationship with another person it is important to come to terms with the relationship we are having with ourselves.

We draw to us things that resonate at the same frequency and are in harmony with how we are feeling and thinking. If we wish to change what is showing up in our life we have to change ourselves. We have to change how we feel about things.

Negative feelings often spring from our belief system and judgements which we make about life and living and the people who are showing up in our life.

It is sometimes necessary to bring these beliefs and judgements to the surface of our mind and challenge them. By challenge I mean run them through your mind again and see if they are still serving you.

Ask yourself, are these your own beliefs or have you adopted them from your parents or partner? Have you learned them at school or been taught them in a religious setting?

Ask yourself what life would be like if you chose to change your mind about these beliefs. How would your judgements change; how would you view yourself; how would it affect your self worth and love for yourself?

What would happen if you changed your perspective on life and who you are?—If you were to choose to see everything as an aspect of yourself—without any separation, just an interaction of love expressed?

If all relationships were in actual fact you flowing energy from one aspect of yourself to another, how would that feel?—If you stopped judging yourself and just enjoyed giving your love unconditionally to those that enter your life, knowing that we are all One?

How would you feel if you knew that your soul were just a silent witness to the events in your life?—That your soul is non-changing, eternal and absolute; that it is not in this physical world but part of an eternal continuum of energy which always was, and always will be, the same?

How would you feel if you became aware that the love in your heart was connected to an infinite source which could flow for eternity?

—That to whichever person you gave your love, in the end that love could only come back to you: because you and the other person were operating in the same field of energy which was connecting you both to the same source?

Do you feel you could be strong enough to love yourself and all that shows up in your life? Do you feel you could love yourself so much that your heart overflowed with this love?

Could you start to appreciate your merit, your beauty, your intelligence and grace?—And value the help and healing you bring to others in your work and your living?

How do you think you would feel if you gave yourself permission to start to love yourself—as you are, doing exactly what you are doing, just because you choose to, without judgement?

You can make this choice; you can choose to be happy now in this moment.

If you do decide to make this choice, your whole world will change: your whole perspective on life will flow freer. You will be able to drop your "story"; you will be able to see Life as it truly is: the exchange of loving energy flowing from one to another.

Play till your heart's content in the field of the Self, the oneness of Life and love that is this universe we live in.

76. Thigh Muscle Continues to Atrophy

If you do not use your physical body it becomes weak and experiences atrophy as the muscles wither away.

You know your physical condition better than me, so please only take this advice if you feel it is appropriate.

What I would recommend is to join a yoga class. There are many types of yoga. A beginner's Hatha Yoga class, which will stretch and energize the muscles in a moderate gentle way, could help you a lot.

Yoga is good because you can set your own limits and increase the practice at your own rate.

What I would recommend is doing a little each day and slowly building up to what you feel comfortable with. This will energize and strengthen the muscles in your thighs.

As you build up your physical strength you may wish to progress to an intermediate class, which will teach the Yogic Breath and more advanced postures like the Salutation to the Sun. If you do this three to five times a day, your physical strength will really start to build.

Yoga, which is another word for balance, will align all your bodies—physical, mental and spiritual, clearing blockages in the energy meridians and improving your sense of wellbeing.

If you get very good at yoga, in say three to six months' time, you may want to advance even further and join an Ashtanga Yoga or Power Yoga class, which really heats up the body and clears out the breathing system and cardiovascular system.

If you do this with conscious breathing, and perhaps take up one of the many methods of meditation, your physical, mental and spiritual bodies will really gain a benefit and you will become more self-aware of who and what you are.

This self-knowledge helps to make you aware of some of the major shifts in consciousness that are taking place at the moment. You would rapidly move up to be one of the foremost lightworkers on the planet, leading the way through awareness for all mankind to follow.

77. Weight and the Root Cause of the Problem

There are a few ways we could look at this, but at the end of the day, I think you will find that it comes down to belief systems. A lot of people live their lives feeling there is not enough money, food, love, time, etc.

But, in reality, you are the Life Force from which all these other things spring.

If we look at the world as a whole, quite often the Western world is wasteful with food, while the people in Africa find there is a shortage: it is all about balance and even distribution of resources, not about scarcity.

The same with your own body: you may believe that there is not enough and at the same time be eating too much to build up reserves against the day of a shortage.

What I would suggest to help with this process is to eat with awareness. Pay attention to what you are eating and be aware of your feelings. Do you feel hungry? Do you feel bloated? Are you happy with your body?

Asking yourself these questions and others you may think of, can help you to check that you are receiving the right signals from the body.

Quite a lot of people eat when, in actual fact, they are thirsty and would really like to drink some water. But their body is interpreting the message the same as for food.

Pay attention to the body; check your feelings and emotions and ask, do I really want to eat at this point, or shall I wait for another hour until I am hungry and will enjoy the food more?

Do you pay attention to what you eat? I.e. do you savour the flavours and textures of the food? Do you chew your food properly, paying attention to how you feel as you eat it? Are you eating what your body is asking for?

It is also best to eat a hearty breakfast and lunch, but then to tail off your intake so as to have an empty stomach at bed time. You burn calories fast during the early part of the day and that is when you need to take them in.

Small changes can make all the difference: reduce your portion size by 10% or eat off a smaller plate. Buy mainly foods with 3% or less saturated fats. Eat lots of fresh fruit and vegetables with each meal.

Get lots of exercise, go for a walk three times a week and do new things which help you to feel good and full of life.

Only you can make the difference—by becoming aware of what you are eating and asking, will this help to achieve the goal I have set myself to have a happy, healthy, balanced body and lifestyle?

78. Fate and Destiny

What is the difference, and how do we choose between them?

We have all heard the terms Fate and Destiny, but what is it in life that makes the difference between which one we follow?

Fate is the natural direction our life is heading in. This is happening anyway, whether we are conscious of it or not. It is the natural flow of life, which is set for us in the stars, and is influenced by the others in our life.

We may quite often react negatively to fate and try to swim the opposite way. We are usually not aware of our deeper feelings and our emotions regarding our fate; we feel that life is in control and we are here just to experience the ride.

Destiny is when we bring our will to bear and become conscious of our thoughts, feeling and emotions; where we take an active role in life and use our own innate consciousness and awareness to choose which direction we want our life to flow in.

Following one's destiny is much more proactive: it is exciting and full of joy and happiness, as the universe rewards you with these feelings for the success you are having in fulfilling your destiny.

The way to find your destiny is to become aware of yourself at subtle levels: to feel the faintest impulses of consciousness, in the mind, in your feelings and in your emotions.

You may like to work on these one at a time by becoming aware of your thoughts, dreams and aspirations, using your imagination and visualizing what it is you would really like to create with your life.

Use your subtle feelings to connect to your Self deep within your heart and other energy centres in the body; feel if there are any blockages or restrictions in the flow of your energy. Become aware of these and, using deep breathing, relax and release these blockages so your energy flows more freely and fully.

Become aware of your emotions and look for the positive in what you are being and doing; feel how you react emotionally to the people and places in your life; again, look for the joy and the positive ways to achieve what you would like to create with your life.

When you become conscious of all the subtle influences which are affecting your life you slowly but surely change from having a fate to being conscious of your destiny. It is all about taking an active part in life and being and doing what makes your heart sing.

Use your passion and enthusiasm to enliven your life and bring the sparkle back; see your achievements grow as your thoughts, words and ideas take on material form and become solid and realized in the world.

❧

79. Symbols and Codes: Why We Use Them and What They Mean

Symbols are pictures which we use to give a message to other beings and to those that will come after us. The interpretation of the symbol is very personal and unique to each individual.

Those symbols and codes we take for granted are things like the alphabet we use in our language. Languages and their associated symbols are a living thing.

Nowhere is this more apparent than when watching our children sending text messages to each other on their mobile phones. They have created their own language, which is unique and constantly changing.

They may use different symbols in different orders when talking with a certain friend and change the order and language with another. I suppose this is a little like local dialect in different parts of the country.

The main thing to be aware of is the relationship between the symbols on the surface of language and their meaning and effects on our emotions and feelings. Also, the message can be sent out on many levels.

As we write we send a telepathic message, which is received by the other person instantly. The letter or email will follow later. It is this telepathic message that pre-programmes the other person's emotions and feeling to interpret the message in a certain way and give it its truth.

Symbols are very powerful: as the old saying goes, a picture says a thousand words. It is the intricate matrix of emotions and feeling that is enlivened by a symbol and connects it to your Inner Self. This connection highlights your own truth that you receive from the symbol used.

Last night while I was sleeping I became aware I was receiving lots of symbols. I was quietly watching as thousands of visual images seemed to be being downloaded into my consciousness. Each image was only visible for about a tenth of a second before my awareness moved on to the next image.

I have yet to understand the reason for this download. It appeared to consist mainly of the symbols used by the ancient Egyptians in their wall paintings of animals and various headdresses.

The point being that it is not the symbol that is important; it is its inner meaning for us as an individual. We all have an inner knowledge and belief system which interprets these symbols. This gives meaning and understanding but it is our inner feelings and emotions which give us our truth.

It is this inner connection to Self—that Inner Universal Life Force—that is the seat of our true Inner Knowledge. Our feeling and emotions join the symbols on the surface of life to the inner depth of knowledge which creates our truth and understanding.

It is as though we compare even the smallest symbol to our Inner Universal Knowledge and, through feelings and emotions, make judgements and decisions which give the symbol meaning for us.

The awareness within and our connection to Self, the Universal Life Force, should not be overshadowed too much by our learned beliefs and judgements. It is important to be aware on what level of our awareness we are deciding and acting.

The more we are in tune with our Soul and Universal Life Force the better, as our actions are in tune with the whole universe.

80. You are Truly an Angel, Radiating your Love Wherever you Go

The following affirmation was sent in to me for comment: "I will continue to try and do my own part to alleviate fear which, I feel, is the greatest stumbling block on our collective way towards change."

I would just like to suggest changing a couple of words:

Change "try": I feel when we are trying we are not being ourselves. I feel it is better to be true to yourself and just be who you are.

Change "fear": Fear is the opposite of love; if we honour ourselves and follow our heart's desire, we will be coming from love; and love and fear cannot occupy the same space, as they are opposites.

Also, FEAR—"False Evidence Appearing Real"—cannot appear in the moment of now. Fear arises when we start to project into the future or look back into the past.

Wake up your awareness to really hear, see, touch, taste and smell what is around you in each moment. Life can only be experienced moment by moment. Live each moment fully connected to your environment, fully connected to your loved ones, awake and aware of the beauty in everything.

Use your imagination to create your moments and create them as a reflection of who you are and what you would like to create in that moment. When you are fully present in the moment, all possibilities are open to your imagination to create the greatest expression of who you are.

Release the controls on your energy. Become truly a radiant being. Your heart is full to overflowing with love; it can never run out. Have the confidence just to create and radiate who you are; add your passion and desire to your dreams, and flow freely.

Share your love freely with yourself; when you do this, you are the universe flowing your energy back to yourself. Be on the leading edge of creation and create a really beautiful future for yourself from yourself, by being yourself.

You are truly blessed.

ABOUT GEORGE E LOCKETT—HEALERGEORGE

For the last 32 years I have been focusing on personal development, involving the study of yoga and meditation and turning the attention in on itself.

This process has led me to some amazing realizations about who the person within the body is, and how this individual awareness interacts with the Universal Mind of the Creator God.

About seven years ago I started practising as a Spiritual Healer. I find the connection that I make to the more subtle energies within myself helps with the effectiveness of my Healing work. I have practised in most parts of the UK, taking a stand at Mind, Body and Spirit Fairs around the country and internationally.

I found also that being aware at these subtle levels opens one's awareness to Spirit and allows the communication to take place between one's senses and those people in Spirit that may wish to communicate from the other side of the veil. This ability allows me to work as a Medium in the Spiritualist Churches.

I hope you have enjoyed this "Journey into the Self" and understood a little more of who and what you are being in this lifetime.

Please feel free to visit my website, where you can listen to the Guided Meditations and request Healing.

http://www.healergeorge.com

Thank you until we connect again.

George E Lockett—HealerGeorge